The Teaching Bridge

A Resource Manual for Part-Time Teachers in Today's Colleges and Universities

Norm Oches
Dr. Stella Nkomo

Arizona Mission Press
Davidson

The Teaching Bridge: A Resource Manual for Part-Time Teachers in Today's Colleges and Universities

By Norm Oches and Stella Nkomo

Publisher: Arizona Mission Press
P.O. Box 28
Davidson, NC 28036-0028

Edited by Janet Summers
Cover design by Robert Aulicino

Trademarks: Excel is a registered trademark of Microsoft Corporation. Scantron is a registered trademark of Scantron Corporation. Elmo is a registered trademark of Elmo Manufacturing Corporation.

First Printed July 2000

ISBN 0-9672951-0-6

Printed in the United States of America

10 9 8 7 6 5 4 3 2 1

Contents

Acknowledgements

To Dick Signorelli, Fran Lilly, Ralph Brown, and Mathew Kadackal at the University of North Carolina - Charlotte, whose use of an early draft of the manual in their first classes helped ensure we were meeting the needs of new part-time teachers.

To Richard Zollinger and Lyndall Hare at Central Piedmont Community College, whose advice and counseling were invaluable in providing a community college perspective.

To Denise Clegg at Queens College in Charlotte, NC, who provided thoughtful guidance on working with bookstores, textbook publishers and textbook wholesalers.

To Ray Purdom in the Teaching & Learning Center at UNC-Greensboro for giving us a valuable teaching center perspective.

To Hubert Setzler at the UNC-Charlotte library, whose invaluable computer help made it all seem so easy.

To Burkhard Pollak, our German connection, without whose timely assistance with formatting and layout this manual would not have made it to the first printing.

About the Authors

Norm Oches

Mr. Oches is a part-time instructor of international business in the Bryan School of Business at the University of North Carolina – Greensboro. He has also taught at Queens College and the University of North Carolina – Charlotte, both in Charlotte, North Carolina, as well as at Milwaukee Area Technical College in Milwaukee, Wisconsin. Mr. Oches received his M.B.A. from Kent State University in Ohio and spent 18 years in international business; his most recent corporate position was International Marketing Manager for Briggs & Stratton Corporation. He now spends his time teaching and writing on adult learning and international business topics from his home in Davidson, N.C.

Dr. Stella Nkomo

Dr. Nkomo is professor and former Chair of the Department of Management in the Belk College of Business Administration at the University of North Carolina – Charlotte, where she teaches courses in management and human resource management. She received her Ph.D. from the University of Massachusetts, Amherst. Dr. Nkomo is a recipient of the NationsBank Teaching Excellence Award and was a member of the American Association of Higher Education Teaching Initiative. A former scholar-in-residence at the Mary Ingraham Bunting Institute of Radcliffe College and Harvard University, she is co-author of the textbook, *Applications in Human Resources Management* and several management articles. In addition, she is on the editorial board of several management journals including *Academy of Management Review, Work and Occupations, Organization,* and *Journal of Management Education.* Dr. Nkomo is a member of the Board of Governors of the Center for Creative Leadership.

Authors' Note

We wrote this manual because we could not find anything available that we felt really bridged the gap between the part-time instructor and the world of academia. Nor could we find anything that bridged the gap between the part-time instructor and his or her supervisor in today's colleges and universities. This manual is about building bridges. We hope you can use it to build your own bridge to a more satisfying teaching experience.

It has been our experience that when a new teacher picks up this manual for the very first time, he or she has every intention of reading it through from cover to cover. Somewhere along the line however, new teachers get so wrapped up in the experience of teaching that the manual gets put aside while they are fighting other fires. Then, somewhere about a third of the way through the school term, they see the manual sitting on the corner of their bookcase, and they decide to page through it again. And their first reaction is always, "I wish I had read this manual first. That's exactly what I needed to know." From then on this guide becomes a constant teaching companion, a tool they refer to when a problem first arises.

Now, we aren't suggesting that you not read this manual before your first class. On the contrary, the more knowledge you can take with you into the classroom, the better off you will be. For example, "Part II, Planning to Save Time" will give you the basic tools you need to get successfully through your first class. What we are suggesting is that you will find parts of this manual more relevant as you get into the actual teaching situation. That's why we've structured it so you can quickly refer back to those parts that have the information you need to solve a specific teaching problem once you have started teaching. Good luck!

Norm Oches
Stella Nkomo

Keeping in Touch!

Teaching. There is no one authority you can turn to, no one source that can show you how to do it better. As a new teacher you are a work-in-process. This manual is a similar work-in-process. We need your input to tell us how well the manual is meeting your needs and how we can improve it to help meet the needs of your fellow teachers and administrators in the future. A new Web site is being designed at **www.teachingbridge.com** that will give you a chance to share your comments and questions with others in the teaching field. It will also be a forum through which you can learn what others are doing to be better teachers in today's colleges and universities. And, you can always reach us with your questions and comments c/o Arizona Mission Press, P.O. Box 28, Davidson, NC 28036-0028. Or you can email us at HigherEd@bellsouth.net. We look forward to hearing from you.

The Authors

Part I

An Introduction to the World of Part-Time Teachers

Chapter 1

You're a Bridge to Learning!

In this chapter:

Why This Manual Is for You

Teaching is often a passion for those who do it well. It's also a skill that can be learned if approached with an open mind and willingness to master new ways of looking at the learning process. This manual has been developed to make teaching easier and more rewarding for both you and your students.

Time is a precious commodity. Part-time teachers are often paid only for the time they spend in the classroom, not for the "prep" (preparation) time needed to get ready for classes. This manual is designed to:

- Save you precious time.

- Provide you with the tools to make every minute spent in and out of the classroom as productive as possible.

- Provide you with the structure to make the most effective use of your time and talents.

In this manual we will review some of the tasks teachers think about as the new school term approaches. For instance, syllabi have to be generated, lesson plans designed, and textbooks ordered. In addition, new part-time teachers will have to ensure they have all the information they need from their schools to do an effective job. This all has to be completed before the first student raises his or her hand with the first question.

What's a teacher?

In this manual we refer to you, to ourselves, and to those who want to be like us as "teachers." Some people reading this may be offended that we are not using a more professional term like "instructor" or "faculty member" to refer to those who teach. Our intention is not to offend, but to elevate. We are using the word teacher in the broadest sense of the word; that is, to refer to a person whose job it is to help others acquire knowledge. People who are teachers also have any number of formal titles they assume because of the institutional structure within which they teach, and we recognize that fact.

In using the word teacher to refer to you and your colleagues we are not intending to infer any particular title or position. In fact, we are trying to avoid using any limiting titles. In calling you a teacher, we only wish to call attention to a vocation, the craft of teaching in its full and most holistic sense. Simply put, a teacher teaches.

The basics and more

Because part-time teachers enter the academic world with all levels of experience in teaching, we have included in this manual some basic tips (for example, which color chalk or marker is most effective, how to make an overhead, etc.) as well as more sophisticated assistance. Our intent is to provide as broad a picture of the teaching world as possible. If some of the information is too basic for you, just skip over it. More in-depth information follows.

How This Manual Is Organized

In addition to the introductory material provided in this section of the manual (Part I) and the resource material in the appendix (Part V), the information in the remaining sections is divided into three major sub-parts (Parts II, III, and IV). Each one addresses what you should be focusing on before, during, and after your class.

II: Before class – planning

Planning for the part-time teacher is even more important than it is for the full-time teacher. Full-time teachers use their teaching skills almost every day of the week. Part-time teachers, on the other hand, have to constantly switch back and forth between the academic world and the non-academic workplace. If there is no structure around which teaching activity is organized, the result may be a poorly focused classroom experience for both the teacher and the student.

III: During class – teaching

Good teaching requires effective communication. Without effective communication, motivating students to learn is next to impossible. For the part-time teacher, basic teaching techniques enhance the communication process and help students absorb material more effectively. Besides reviewing the basic skills needed in the classroom, this part of the manual provides teaching tips that will make the experience more fulfilling for both you and the student.

IV: After class – evaluating

One of the most time-consuming parts of the teaching process, for both full- and part-time teachers, is evaluating students. If a basic set of objectives is not laid down early in the process, the evaluation experience can be fraught with indecision and uncertainty. We will review different options that you can use in your own classroom to evaluate students. You can then decide which method works best for you.

How To Find Help in This Manual

We recognize that teachers at many different kinds of colleges and universities will be using this manual. We also recognize that some of these schools will be on the quarter system and others on the semester system. To simplify matters, we have chosen some general terms to represent vocabulary that can change from school to school. For instance, we use the word "school" throughout this manual when describing the place where teaching and learning takes place and the words "term" and "school term," the teaching period covered. We use the term "department head" to mean department chair, program director, or whomever part-time teachers report to at your school. And finally, because the terms "part-time" teacher and "adjunct" teacher are often used interchangeably, we will use the term part-time teacher to refer to any teacher who is not a full-time faculty member at a community college or who is not a tenured or tenure-track faculty member at a four-year college, graduate college, or university.

Teaching tips

Wherever possible we will give you some tips to help make your teaching job a little easier. Each teaching tip will begin with an icon with "TIP" in the center. The subject of the TIP will follow in a stylized font. For example, later in this manual you'll learn how to create lecture notes from computer-generated chapter outlines. A corresponding TIP might be:

Lecture Notes: **You can easily create your own lecture notes by adding a number of spaces between each line of the chapter outline and writing your own notes in that space.**

These helpful hints will also alert you to some of the common mistakes new teachers make or some of the critical things new teachers need to know to avoid future problems. Where we feel a word to the wise is necessary, you will find an icon with "ALERT" in the center. Following will be the subject of the ALERT and the text. For example, you'll learn about the demands on your time that changing textbooks will make. A corresponding ALERT might be:

Changing Textbooks: **If you do plan to change your textbook, do it over the summer when you have more time. Changing a textbook between school terms only compounds the work involved in updating your notes, revising overheads, etc. And remember, changing textbooks can also add to the cost of your students' college education. When you change textbooks, students may find that used books are not available for your new choice.**

Appendix and Index

At the end of this manual you will find an Appendix full of additional resources you can use to help you be a better teacher. In addition, we have designed the index to make it easy for you to find the information you need quickly.

Your Journey Over the Bridge

Although this manual has information that anyone in the teaching profession will find useful, it is designed primarily to meet the needs of part-time teachers who are entering academia after having spent time practicing their craft outside of the academic setting. This includes businesspeople, nurses, technicians and anyone else who wants to pass on some of their expertise to students in technical schools, community colleges, four-year, and graduate universities. This manual is designed to help bridge the teaching and non-teaching worlds more effectively, to help new teachers become more familiar with the ins and outs of the academic environment, and to help new teachers develop the skills that will make them more effective teachers right from the start.

 Quick Reference Tool: When reading this manual you'll find information that you want to be able to refer back to quickly once your class begins. Take a regular 1½" x 2" Post-it® note, turn it upside down, and put a notation on the top edge as a reference. Then stick it on the page you want to refer back to with the non-stick part (and your note) sticking out past the edge of the page.

The Teaching Environment

Many of you will be teaching in an environment with which you have not had contact for many years. Understanding how the environment is structured will help you better deal with it.

In essence, schools are basically made up of students, administrators and teachers. There is often a pecking order among a school's part- and full-time teaching staff. What that pecking order is will be heavily influenced by the type of school in question, for example, community college, a four-year college, or a research university.

There is also a pecking order among students. For instance, in the eyes of most teachers, seniors are a notch above freshmen and sophomores while graduate students are several notches above any of their undergraduate colleagues, and so on. And, although there is a pecking order that exists between all levels of students, it is most pronounced, at least in the eyes of teachers, between undergraduate and graduate level students. As you might imagine, the general attitude towards learning, and to thinking analytically, is more developed in graduate students than in undergraduates.

Once you understand the academic system you will have a better idea of how you and your skills fit into the grand scheme of things at your school. You will learn which courses are the best prerequisites for your course and how your course complements other courses. You will learn how your teaching style meshes with that of the other faculty. And you will come to understand what is the best method for teaching your course to meet the needs of both the students in your class and the administrators to whom you report.

To help you understand how their systems work, schools provide college catalogs, student and faculty handbooks, and similar printed material to guide you through the process. Use the checklists in Chapter 2 to find out what materials are available at your particular school. Many schools also offer new-teacher orientation sessions that can help acclimate you to the academic environment at your school. Ask if your department holds such orientation sessions for its new teachers.

Part-time vs. full-time

The world of the part-time teacher is markedly different from that of the full-time faculty member. Teaching is often the only task a part-time teacher is responsible for. It is often the only one they are paid for as well. Part-time teachers are seldom compensated for the time they spend outside the classroom reviewing textbooks, building lesson plans, grading papers, etc. Teaching assistants/graduate assistants can also be thought of as part-time teachers since teaching is not there only priority, nor are they considered full-time, tenure track faculty.

Besides teaching, full-time faculty must develop curriculum, attend meetings, do research, and advise students. At four-year schools and research institutions, teaching may have to take a back seat to research and other non-teaching activities for full-time teachers to meet tenure requirements or promotion goals. We will discuss some of the more important differences between full-time and part-time teachers later in the manual.

Your first priority: information

If you are a part-time teacher, teaching is usually your primary responsibility. An important secondary responsibility in the weeks before and just after your class begins is to get as much information as you can about your school and the skills and support material you will need to be effective in the classroom. Few schools have all the information available from one source and the responsibility often falls on the part-time teacher to find the information he or she needs. In Chapter 2 you will find checklists which prompt you for the information you will need to collect.

It can get a little lonely out there

Your full-time colleagues are in constant contact with the school administration and their fellow full-time teachers. For them, teaching is only a part of the academic social structure. For the part-time teacher, on the other hand, teaching is often a solitary experience. You will be preparing your material, leading your class, and evaluating your class's work…all alone. To get the most out of the teaching experience, it's important that you contact other teachers and administrators and learn about their teaching experiences and techniques.

You will often find that full-time teachers will not seek you out to learn more about your teaching skills and the experiences you've had in your chosen field. They have their own responsibilities to deal with. Often they are under pressure to finish a book or research project. In essence, you will be working in a parallel universe to your full-time colleagues – part of the academic environment, but not fully part of it. If you can accept this reality and move on with a positive attitude, then you are ahead of the game. If your school has a mentoring program for new teachers, use it to become more connected to the academic life at your school. Check to see if your school has a teaching center and how you can take advantage of the programs and services offered there.

Students

As you might expect, students come in all shapes, sizes, and colors. From an administrative point of view, students are often categorized as follows:

Community College	Undergraduate	Graduate
A. Curriculum	A. Freshman	A. Post-graduate
B. Continuing Ed	B. Sophomore	B. Master's
	C. Junior	C. Doctoral
	D. Senior	D. Post-doctoral

Most professors and department heads know their livelihood depends to a great degree on meeting the needs of students. Your students may be looking for more practical applications of the material presented than might have been true when you went to school. Many students today are putting themselves through school and will want to know how your course will pay off for them in the future. A recent study by UCLA's Higher Education Research Institute (Sax, Astin, Korn, & Mahoney 1998) shows that 77 per cent of college freshmen enter college "to be able to get a better job." This is in comparison to only 62 per cent who are in school "to gain a general education and appreciation of ideas."

A disturbing statistic is that many of the students coming into today's colleges and universities do so with poorer study habits than did their counterparts just 15 years ago. Thirty-three per cent of the college freshmen entering schools in 1998 say they studied or did homework six or more hours a week during their senior year in high-school. This is in comparison to a figure of 44 per cent when the same question was asked back in 1987.

With these statistics in mind, students are still expecting teachers to be better at what they do – teach.

Administrators

Although the specific terms vary from school to school, the administrator you will probably meet first, and who will often be the one who recommends you be hired, is the department or program "head." Other titles used for this function are department chair, program chair, program coordinator, and program director, to name a few. This department or program head is responsible for a specific subject area such as marketing, English, engineering technology, community nursing, etc., within a "school," "college" or "department" (School of Business, College of Arts & Sciences, Engineering School, Nursing School, Department of Continuing Education, etc.). Along with running a department, department heads are often expected to teach one or more courses in their subject area. Usually, the department head will need to get final approval to hire you from the dean or division director of the school or college. It is the dean or division director who normally has budgetary authority when it comes to hiring part-time teachers, but it is usually the department or program head who makes the actual hiring decision. This is the person who would normally be your supervisor or mentor.

In making the decision to hire you, your department head has had to consider the constraints of curriculum requirements, scheduling, class size, and procedural limitations imposed by the school. He or she may have already decided such things for you as:

- Class meeting time (day or evening).
- The days of the week the class will meet.
- Class size limit.
- The particular prerequisites that need to be fulfilled before a student can register for the class.

Department heads also decide whether you will be hired back.

Throughout this manual we have chosen to use the term "department head" to represent the person who is your supervisor and who has most likely made the decision to hire you. The title of the person you actually report to may be different, depending on the school in question and how it is structured. Any of the other terms schools use to refer to departmental or school administration are equally valid.

Be understanding

Today's school administrators are feeling pressure from all sides – from the budget office to cut costs, from the students to provide additional and more efficient services, from parents wanting a better education for their children, and from state and federal legislators who want a more effective system for all. Particularly if you are teaching in a four-year or graduate level college or university and you think your department head is sometimes ignoring you, don't worry, it's not personal. People in these positions have a million fires to put out. If they could spend more time with you, they would. And in fact, most department heads will do their very best to get you started out on the right foot. But the truth is they have to concentrate on supporting their full-time faculty first. Once the school term begins and their administrative workload increases, they are not going to be able to focus much on the problems of part-time teachers.

For those teaching in community colleges and technical school settings, you may find administrators more accessible. This is because the focus of these schools is primarily on teaching and in many cases part-time teachers comprise a majority of the teaching staff.

Teachers

As mentioned earlier, the title "teacher" can be applied to a number of categories of teaching professionals in the academic world. A teacher can be an "adjunct" or "part-time" teacher who teaches only one or two classes a term. The adjunct or part-time teacher usually has to have a minimum degree level (masters, M.B.A., etc.) and a minimum number of hours of post-graduate work in the discipline he or she will be teaching. Usually they are only allowed to teach students who have degrees one or more steps lower than their own. For example, someone with an M.B.A. would not be allowed to teach students in an M.B.A. program, but would be allowed to teach undergraduate and community college courses.

A teacher can also be an adjunct instructor who teaches full-time, but is hired on a contractual basis, not on the basis of a "tenure track" selection. The term teacher is also applied to full-time, tenured, and tenure track (working to qualify for tenure) professors.

In the strictest sense of the word the term "adjunct" refers to a teacher who signs up to teach a certain number of classes and is given a contract for a certain period of time (at a set salary). These teachers are often not on a tenure track to becoming "full" professors. Some four-year and graduate institutions hire adjunct professors to teach a full-time course load where there is a lack of expertise in the existing faculty or a temporary teaching position that needs filling. A part-time faculty member often teaches only one or two classes per term and is usually paid per course.

In many schools the academic classification of teachers is as follows (from highest to lowest in rank):

Four-year colleges and universities	**Community colleges**
1. Full professor	1. Full-time instructor/faculty
2. Associate professor	2. Part-time/adjunct instructor
3. Assistant professor	3. Trainer/facilitator
4. Instructor/lecturer	
5. Adjunct instructor	
6. Part-time instructor	

In community colleges, where much of the teaching staff is drawn from the community (and tenure is not the issue it is at four-year schools), there is not as perceived a difference between part-time and full-time positions as you find in four-year schools.

In four-year institutions the key variable that determines a teacher's status is whether he or she is tenured or non-tenured.

Teachers can be classified as a:

1. Tenured full professor
2. Tenured associate professor
3. Non-tenured assistant professor on tenure track
4. Non-tenure track instructor (full-time adjunct with no tenure prospects)

In many four-year and research institutions professors hired at entry level have seven years to "make" tenure. If they are not accepted for tenure within that period of time, they have to leave that school and try to make tenure at another school. Or they may have to look for a position outside of academia. Non-tenure track, full-time adjuncts who do not have the required terminal degree to teach as full-time tenured professors might be called "visiting professors," special "chair" professors, or simply "instructors."

How other teachers see you

You may find that some full-time faculty members at four-year schools resent the fact that part-time teachers are teaching in place of what should be (in their minds) a full-time, tenured or tenure-track faculty position. Since most part-time teachers do not have to take on the day-to-day non-teaching activities that are part of a full-time professor's job description (e.g. student advising, office hours, etc.), some full-time professors feel they, the full-time professors, are unfairly having to take on additional work without being reasonably compensated. They might have a point if part-time teachers were "reasonably" compensated for the time they spend outside the classroom developing lessons, grading papers, etc. Fortunately, this negative view of part-time teachers is waning as the need to cut costs becomes more apparent and the need to fill vacant teaching positions becomes more acute.

A L E R T

Accreditation: Some school accreditation organizations (see below) insist that a certain percentage of course work in four year and graduate institutions be taught by full-time teachers. This restricts, to some degree, the number of part-time teachers a school can hire and still be accredited by their accrediting organization.

Finding Your Focus: Talk with faculty members who are teaching courses that either precede or follow yours and learn what their course objectives are. In this way, you can avoid any duplication of effort. The process is also a good way to begin building relationships with other faculty members.

Accreditation Boards

Today, many academic departments must satisfy criteria established by one or more accrediting organizations, for example, the American Assembly of Collegiate Schools of Business (AACSB) or the National Council for Accreditation of Teacher Education (NCATE). The goal of these organizations is to give parents, students, and administrators the means to evaluate schools according to whether the school has or has not met the criteria of a particular accrediting organization. You might want to ask your supervisor what accrediting organization(s) your department belongs to and what effect, if any, this will have on your evaluation as a teacher.

In addition to meeting accreditation criteria, most schools are classified according to the Carnegie Classification System.

1. **Associate's** (one level only): Schools offer associate of arts, certificate, or degree programs, but do not offer baccalaureate (four-year) degrees. This is the category in which most community colleges are placed.

2. **Baccalaureate** (levels I and II): Primarily undergraduate colleges with a major emphasis on baccalaureate degree programs.

3. **Master's** (levels I and II): Schools offering a full range of courses in a baccalaureate program as well as commitment to graduate education through a master's degree program.

4. **Doctoral** (levels I and II): Schools offering a full range of courses in a baccalaureate program as well as commitment to graduate education through the doctoral level.

5. **Research** (levels I and II): Schools offering a full range of courses in a baccalaureate program, commitment to graduate education through the doctoral level, and a high priority placed on research.

6. **Professional Schools and Specialized Institutions** (one level only): Schools that award degrees from bachelor's to doctoral, primarily in specialized fields such as theology, medicine, law, engineering, teaching, etc.

7. **Tribal Colleges and Universities** (one level only): Schools located primarily on reservations and controlled by American Indian educational organizations.

The Changing Academic Environment

In the community college environment, teaching is and always has been the primary component of the teacher's job description. For many four-year and research institutions, teaching has had to take a backseat in importance to scholarly research. Teaching is something done to get a paycheck. It is research and publications that enhance a four-year or research institution's prestige within the academic community and, as a result, bring in much-needed funding.

Fortunately today, many schools are reevaluating their focus on research and finding ways to re-emphasize the importance of good teaching. Some of this change is being driven by the move to "smart classrooms" (computer enhanced) and "distance learning." An increase in the number and quality of college and university "teaching centers" (see Appendix) is an indication of this renewed interest in teaching quality. As teaching takes a place alongside research as a primary focus of a school's mission in the academic community, good teachers, whether full- or part-time, will find their services in greater demand than ever before.

Even if you find you are teaching at a school where classroom instruction takes a back seat to research, you can still make a major impact by being a good teacher and investing as much of your time as you can in motivating your students to do their best.

Your research: There are two kinds of "research" that take place in schools today. There is academic research that a teacher carries out in his or her field to further the understanding of the subject area in the academic community. This is the same research a teacher completes to meet tenure requirements and to help the school meet accreditation criteria. Part-time teachers are seldom asked to do this kind of research. A second kind of research is the research that is done to ensure that teachers are fully informed concerning the most up-to-date information in their field and are ready to address these topics in class. This is called "academic preparation." You will be responsible for carrying out this second kind of research on your own. The Internet is an incredible resource for gathering the latest information on your subject area. Public and college libraries can also help. And, academic journals will give you an idea of what others in academia are writing and thinking about in your subject area.

The Computer – In and Out of the Classroom

The computer and the Internet are having a profound effect not only on how information is being presented in the classroom, but on the very structure of higher education itself. Computer-assisted instruction is gradually becoming a part of many schools' standard procedure in the classroom. In addition, computer networks within schools are supporting the dissemination of information between students and professor. The next wave of progress is just around the corner in the form of distance learning, where a school no longer requires bricks and mortar to exist, but can exist in its own corner of cyberspace. In distance learning, students log onto the Internet, and at their own pace take courses that fit into their busy schedules. This is particularly important with the number of older students coming back to school to update their skills, to reengineer their careers, or to take courses that will hold their interest into retirement.

The computer is going to change how colleges and universities do business. And it will affect how they use part-time teachers as well. It is not improbable that at some time in the future students will be taking courses on the Web and use teachers (both part- and full-time) as subject matter experts to help them with material that only becomes relevant through interaction with an actual practitioner. For more information on instructional technology and how it can be used to enhance your teaching, see Chapter 9.

Personal and Professional Issues

Teacher training

It is often a surprise when part-time teachers first learn that many of their full-time colleagues in higher education have never had any formal training on how to teach. Many have followed a very arduous program to meet the requirements of study in their field, but few have had any formal courses in how to translate their knowledge into active student learning. Some full-time faculty had a chance to get their feet wet in the classroom while acting as teaching assistants in their graduate programs, but often without any formal training involved. This means that most have had to learn it as they go along, just like you are doing now. Fortunately, many colleges and universities are now opening teaching centers (see Appendix) to help their faculty make the transition from school to classroom a little smoother. So, don't feel so bad if you don't get it right the first time. You are going through the same process that your full-time colleagues had to go through to become effective teachers.

Find a mentor

Probably the most effective way to become a more integral part of the academic environment is to have a mentor "on the inside." Whether it is a department chair, a full-time professor who teaches in your discipline, or a curriculum coordinator, having such a mentor will help you feel more comfortable in the academic environment.

You have a big responsibility

If you truly want to be an effective teacher, learn all the teaching skills you can before you step into the classroom. This manual is a first step. But, even with the best preparation, you are going to make some mistakes. And making a couple of mistakes is not a sin. But making the same mistake over and over can have a far-reaching effect on every student in your class. It's up to you, and to you alone, to walk through that classroom door well prepared and ready to nurture the learning process.

Be gentle on yourself

Don't let what's happening in a particular class get you down. There will be days when you say something brilliant to a roomful of young faces and are rewarded with looks as blank as the wall at your back. Keep your sense of humor. If you're trying to do the best job possible, that's all your students or your school can ask of you. Listen to what your students say, and more importantly, what they don't say. You will learn to recognize the signs that learning is taking place. Many schools have students fill out teacher evaluation forms near the end of each term (see Chapter 6). Use teacher evaluations as a tool to help you improve your teaching skills. And don't depend only on feedback from your students and peers. Use your evaluation tools (such as tests, projects, etc.) to find out if you are truly doing a good job. If students don't understand the material, a well-structured test will confirm it.

The world's greatest excuses

You'll need to exercise some degree of skepticism as you begin your teaching career. Today's teachers face a generation of students who, in some cases, have never had to be accountable for anything. Therefore, when it comes to late homework and missed classes you'll hear every excuse in the book, and some that haven't been invented yet. Be prepared.

My Grade: **Many student complaints boil down to one major theme: "The teacher didn't give me the right grade." It will be up to you to let students know a teacher does not give anything, but that grades are something they earn.**

So You Want To Be Full-time!

Some people start out teaching part-time hoping that it will lead to a full-time position. If you are one of those people, then you have some major challenges ahead of you. For one thing, if you do not have a doctorate in your field, it's going to be very difficult for you to find a full-time position in a four-year college or university. This is particularly true for schools that are looking to upgrade their curriculum by hiring only those candidates with terminal degrees (Ph.D.), and then, only those from the top tier schools. Many four-year and research institutions feel they have a reputation in the academic community they have to maintain, accreditation standards to achieve, and a product image in the community that must be upheld. And, there are a lot of out-of-work Ph.D.s looking for the same position you want.

So what kind of full-time positions can you reasonably hope to find? If you teach something that no one else has expertise in, it may open up to a full-time position, but only if the school is large enough to support more than one section of your course. The reason a person with a niche expertise is so popular as a part-time teacher is the very reason that a full-time teaching position is not often available. It's a niche subject that attracts a small number of students. If it were a broad interest course, universities would be turning out enough Ph.D.s to meet the demand for it. The message here is that if you want to teach in a four-year or research institution, go get a Ph.D. or similar terminal degree. Even if you did get a full-time, non-tenure position without a Ph.D., you will never have job security since your contract must be renewed annually and your position could be upgraded at any time (with a Ph.D. hired to fill the position).

There is another way to use your special expertise to obtain a teaching position. Endow a chair. That is, make a contribution to a school that will help support future candidates after you have left. It's an expensive way to go, but if you have the resources, it's one way to get hired full-time. Or, if you have the expertise and name recognition in your field you may be able to take over one of these endowed chair positions.

Or, you could teach at a community college full time. This is a real possibility, although you have to remember that community colleges depend on part-timers to fill a good portion of their teaching positions. Community colleges often look for teachers willing to teach night courses, a niche where community colleges fill a very real need in the community. So, if you are willing to teach nights, this is a possibility. You also might catch the eye of a community college administrator and be hired full-time to teach days and nights. A challenge in all these cases is that community college professors are often overworked and underpaid, so you need to be willing to take a salary that is in many cases less than or equal to that of a high school teacher.

Another possibility is to take a full-time administrative staff position within a college or university and teach one or two courses while holding down a full-time administrative position. You would still be part of the college community, although not as a full-time teacher.

The message is that using part-time teaching as a stepping stone to a full-time position is not a viable strategy in many cases, although there are always exceptions. Know what you are getting into before making the decision to use a part-time position to look for a full-time one. You may be barking up the wrong tree.

Why Teaching Can Be its Own Reward

Good adjunct and part-time teachers can turn the sometimes-bland world of academic theory into an exciting world of reality for their students. On the other hand, poor adjunct and part-time teachers can turn a class into nothing more than a never ending series of war stories, leaving no solid foundation upon which students can build their careers. More than ever, students need their own bridge to the world outside the classroom that only actual practitioners like you can provide. And school administrators need you too! Schools are increasingly turning to part-time teachers as budgets tighten and they look for ways to stretch their education dollars. It's the right time, and it's the right place.

After all is said and done, teaching will probably be the most rewarding thing you ever do. Seeing the light of understanding come on in students' eyes, a light that you have lit, is a feeling like no other. Good luck and may the next student you turn on to your subject be the one who changes a thousand other lives.

NOTES:

_____

_____

_____

_____

_____

_____

_____

_____

_____

_____

Part II

Getting Ready

Chapter 2

Planning for Success

In this chapter:

Me, Plan? Who's Got the Time?

As in any part of today's hectic life, you need to plan to make the best use of finite resources – in this case your time and your abilities. Good planning is even more critical for part-time teachers than for full-time teachers. Why? As a part-time teacher you spend much of your workweek outside of the classroom. On the day of your class you return to the classroom and try to take up where you left off at the end of the last class session. Sometimes it is difficult to keep the classroom discussion flowing smoothly from one class to another. Effective planning ensures you won't have to waste time at the beginning of each class session trying to remember what was discussed in the previous class, what needs to be discussed in this class, and what remains to be discussed in the future.

War-story-itis

One of the major benefits of using part-time teachers is that they can relate classroom material to the world outside the classroom. Unfortunately, a common complaint is that part-time teachers spend too much time telling war stories and not enough time helping students understand the material they will need to pass the next exam, meet the prerequisites of the next course, or get a job. Planning helps you balance the use of structured course material with real-life experiences.

End rush

New teachers tend to run out of time at the end of the school term, which forces them to rush through critical material or leave it out of the class discussions altogether. Planning helps distribute the material to be covered throughout the term so the right amount of material is discussed each week.

So, What Do We Mean by Planning?

Good planning is the key to a successful classroom experience for both you and your students. Like any other process, planning requires that you do some minimal amount of research up front. This should include the following:

- Carefully reading the textbook that will be used in your course.

- Reviewing other textbooks available on the subject you are teaching.

- Reviewing articles that discuss current topics in your subject area.

- Asking for input from others who have taught your course in the past.

- Reviewing old syllabi for your course or courses similar to yours.

- Planning activities both in and out of the classroom that will help motivate students to learn. For example, using a guest lecturer, Internet assignments, trips to the library, etc.

- Obtaining the administrative information you need from your department head, mentor, and other school administrators to carry out your responsibilities as a teacher.

Checklists to Plan With!

The checklists that follow will help you collect the information you need to function effectively as a teacher in your school. Some of the information you need will be standard across all schools and subject areas. Other information will be unique to your school or your subject area. You will need to meet with your department head and/or mentor as soon as you have been hired to begin gathering the necessary information.

Initial Contacts

To begin the process of gathering information you will probably meet with your department head and/or his or her administrative assistant. This checklist will help you keep track of the names and positions of people you meet as you begin the information gathering process.

Contact: _____

Position: _____ Phone: _____

Contact: _____

Position: _____ Phone: _____

Contact: _____

Position: _____ Phone: _____

Contact: _____

Position: _____ Phone: _____

NOTES: _____

_____

_____

_____

_____

_____

_____

_____

_____

Printed/Online Resources

Use the following checklist to determine what catalogs, handbooks, etc. are available that will provide you with information you need to carry out your responsibilities as a teacher:

✔ Faculty handbook

Contact: _____ Phone: _____

Email Address: _____

✔ Part-time faculty handbook

Contact: _____ Phone: _____

Email Address: _____

✔ Student handbook

Contact: _____ Phone: _____

Email Address: _____

✔ Course catalog

Contact: _____ Phone: _____

Email Address: _____

✔ Class schedule

Contact: _____ Phone: _____

Email Address: _____

✔ Exam schedule

Contact: _____ Phone: _____

Email Address: _____

✔ Campus phone/email directory

Contact: _____ Phone: _____

Email Address: _____

Printed/Online Resources (cont'd)

✓ Other: _____

   Contact: _____ Phone: _____

   Email Address: _____

✓ School's home page Internet address:

_____

NOTES:

_____

_____

_____

_____

_____

_____

_____

_____

_____

_____

_____

_____

_____

_____

_____

_____

_____

_____

_____

_____

_____

_____

_____

Course Information

Use the following checklist to gather the information on your particular course as well as some basic information on the students who will be taking the course:

✓ Course title: _____

_____

✓ Course number: _____

✓ Section number: _____

✓ Meeting day and time:

Day: M T W Th F Sa Su (circle)

Time: _____ to _____

Other: _____

✓ Course level (estimated % of class that might be juniors, seniors, etc.):

Freshman ___% Sophomore ___% Junior ___%

Senior ___% Graduate ___% Other: _____ ___%

✓ Credit hours: _____

✓ Classroom number: _____ Building: _____

✓ Course description: _____

_____

_____

_____

✓ Class size (if not available, ask for average): _____

✓ Prerequisite courses:

1. _____

2. _____

Course Information (cont'd)

✓ Other faculty who have taught the course in the past:

Contact: _____ Phone: _____

Contact: _____ Phone: _____

NOTES:

_____

_____

_____

_____

_____

_____

_____

_____

_____

_____

_____

_____

_____

_____

_____

_____

_____

_____

_____

_____

_____

_____

Instructor Logistics

Use the following checklist to gather the information on office, mailbox, keys, and other assets you may have at your disposal:

✓ **Office:** Will I have an office?

If yes:

Building name/number? _____

Office number? _____

Do I share the office?

If yes, with whom? _____

Where do I get keys/security code for my office?

Contact: _____ Phone: _____

Where do I get keys/security code for the building?

Contact: _____ Phone: _____

Days/hours building is open? _____

✓ **Phone:** Will I have a phone?

If yes, what is phone number? ( ) _____

If shared, with whom? _____

Is the number the same as the department secretary's?

If yes, what is secretary's name? _____

Has he/she been notified I will be using his/her phone?

_____

If no phone is available, is there a campus phone number I can refer students to? ( ) _____

Instructor Logistics (cont'd)

✓ **Mailbox:**

Mailbox number/name/location:

_____

_____

When are mailboxes accessible (day, night, weekend)?

_____

Mailbox address for mail coming from off campus:

_____

_____

Should I use interoffice mailing envelopes for sending documents to other school staff?

If yes, where can I get them?

_____

Instructions for using mailing envelopes:

_____

_____

Who is the contact person for questions about the mailbox?

Contact: _____ Phone:_____

✓ **Computer:** Will I have the use of a computer?

If yes, where is it located? _____

Where is printer located? _____

How do I sign onto the system?_____

_____

_____

_____

Instructor Logistics (cont'd)

Where can I get technical assistance should I have a problem with my computer?

Contact: _____ Phone: _____

✓ **Email:** Will I have a school email address?

If yes, how do I obtain the address? _____

_____

My email address will be/is:

_____

What is the name of the email system at this school?

_____

What is the location of computer access to my email account (if not on my office computer)?

_____

How do I log on to the email system from school?

_____

_____

Can I log on to the email system from my home or office? If yes, how?

_____

_____

✓ **Copying:** Where is the photocopier located?

Location: _____

Do I need a copy card to use the copier? _____

Contact: _____ Phone: _____

Do I need a security code to use the copier?

Code: _____

Instructor Logistics (cont'd)

✓ **ID Card:** Where can I obtain an ID card?

Contact: _____   Phone: _____

✓ **Parking:**
Where can I park?

Lot number(s): _____   Location: _____

_____

Where can I get a parking permit?

Location: _____

Contact: _____   Phone: _____

Other parking info I should know? _____

_____

NOTES:

_____

_____

_____

_____

_____

_____

_____

_____

_____

_____

_____

_____

_____

Syllabus

Use the following checklist to determine what assistance is available to help you develop and distribute your class syllabus:

✓ Will the departmental support staff type the syllabus for me?
   If yes, who?
   Contact: _____ Phone: _____

✓ Who is responsible for making copies of the syllabus for my class?
   Contact: _____ Phone: _____

   If I am responsible, where can I get copies made?

   _____

✓ To whom am I to send a copy of my syllabus when it is completed
   (e.g. department head or chair, department secretary, etc.)?

   1. _____

   2. _____

   3. _____

   By what date?   Mo. _____ Day_____ Yr._____

   Hard copy, diskette, or email? _____

✓ Does this school have a recommended syllabus format?

   If yes, where can I find it? _____

   If no, is there another syllabus I can use as a guide?

   _____

✓ Items that the school <u>requires</u> be included in my syllabus:

   1. _____

   2. _____

   3. _____

Syllabus (cont'd)

✓ Other items I might want to include in my syllabus:

1. _____

2. _____

3. _____

✓ Source(s) for copies of syllabi from other teachers at this school:

Contact: _____ Phone: _____

Contact: _____ Phone: _____

✓ Is there a course coordinator or curriculum coordinator who can tell me more about my course and any requirements I may need to meet?

Contact: _____ Phone: _____

NOTES:

_____

_____

_____

_____

_____

_____

_____

_____

_____

_____

_____

_____

_____

_____

_____

_____

Textbook Choice

Your textbook may already have been chosen for you. However, if this is not the case, you will need to quickly choose one. This checklist will help you determine whether you have to choose a text and if so, what the procedure is for doing so. Chapter 3, "Choosing a Textbook," walks you through the actual process of choosing a textbook using the information below.

✓Who is normally responsible for choosing the textbook?

_____

✓Has the textbook already been selected?

If yes, which text has been selected?

Title: _____

ISBN number: _____

Number ordered: _____

Cost: _____

Why was this book chosen? _____

_____

Where can I obtain a desk copy and instructor's manual for this book?

_____

If no, what forms do I have to fill out to select a textbook?

Form: _____

Contact: _____ Phone: _____

Who is responsible for forwarding the selection to the bookstore?

Contact: _____ Phone: _____

By what date do I have to choose a textbook?

Mo. _____ Day_____ Yr._____

Textbook Choice (cont'd)

How many copies do I need to order? _____

To whom can I look for guidance in choosing a textbook?

_____

✓ Is this class part of a series of classes that deals with my subject area?

If yes, what other textbooks do I need to review in this series to ensure that the textbook I choose meets the content requirements of the series?

1. _____

2. _____

3. _____

✓ Whom can I contact at the bookstore should I have any questions concerning the textbook selection process?

Contact: _____ Phone: _____

NOTES:

_____

_____

_____

_____

_____

_____

_____

_____

_____

_____

_____

_____

Evaluation

Use the following checklist to ensure that you have all the information you need to develop your evaluation system:

✓ Where can I find a final exam schedule? _____

_____

✓ Final grades are due on? Date: ___/___/___ Time: _____

How soon after giving final exam must final grades be

turned in? _____

✓ To whom do they go? _____

✓ Is there a school-wide grading policy?
  If yes, what is the policy? _____

  _____

  If no, can anyone give me any advice on how to develop a
  grading system? _____

  _____

✓ Is there a school-wide grading scale?

  If yes, what is it? _____

  _____

✓ Can I obtain a review of the grading history for the course (or
  related courses) I am going to be teaching?

  If yes, who can supply it?

  Contact: _____ Phone: _____

✓ Is there a grade point range for this course (or related courses)
  that the school would like me to be aware of when determining
  the final grades for my students?
  If yes, what is it? _____

  If no, can you suggest an appropriate target range?

  Between _____ and _____

Evaluation (cont'd)

✔ Is there a school-wide attendance policy?

  If yes, what is it?_____

  _____

  If no, how do other faculty evaluate attendance?

  _____

✔ Is there a dismissal policy for students who sign up for the course, but do not attend the first class?

  _____

✔ What form(s) do I use to alert the school when a student consistently misses class or does not attend at all?

  Form: _____

NOTES:

_____

_____

_____

_____

_____

_____

_____

_____

_____

_____

_____

_____

_____

Technology

Use the following checklist to locate the communication technology resources at your school:

✓ Does the school have a campus-wide email system?

   If yes, does every student have access? _____

✓ What information do students normally receive from their teachers via email?

   1. _____

   2. _____

   3. _____

   4. _____

✓ Do teachers in this school use on-line discussion groups or chat rooms as teaching tools?

   _____

✓ Are there any restrictions on the use of the Internet by students?

   _____

✓ Are there any minimum computer competency requirements for students attending this school?

   _____

✓ What is the general level of computer competency among students in this department?

   Excellent   Good   Fair   Poor

✓ Are computer labs available for students' general use?
   If yes, where are they located?

   _____

Teaching Tools

Use the following checklist to make sure you know what tools are available for use in the classroom:

✓ The following are (circle option beside each choice):
   A. Available in the classroom.
   B. Must be ordered before term begins.
   C. Must be ordered before each class, for each class.

Overhead transparency projector	A	B	C
Visual presentation equipment (e.g., Elmo ®)	A	B	C
Slide projector	A	B	C
Multimedia projector	A	B	C
Projection screen	A	B	C
Video player	A	B	C
Television monitor	A	B	C
Computer for teacher's use	A	B	C
Computers for students' use	A	B	C
Cassette tape player	A	B	C
Other: _____	A	B	C
_____	A	B	C

✓ If equipment must be ordered before each class, or at beginning of term, what is the procedure?

   Contact: _____ Phone: _____

   Procedure: _____

   _____

✓ Whom do I contact about TV and video equipment problems?

   Contact: _____ Phone: _____

Teaching Tools (cont'd)

✔ Whom do I contact about computer questions or problems?

Contact: _____ Phone: _____

Whom do I contact about overhead projector/video and other multimedia equipment questions or problems?

Contact: _____ Phone: _____

Where can I make overhead transparencies (e.g. copier, heat transfer equipment, etc.)? _____

_____

Where are spare bulbs located for the projection equipment?

_____

✔ Regarding general equipment use:
Whom can I call on should I have a problem with any of the equipment I plan to use in my classroom?

Contact: _____ Phone: _____

Hours available: _____ To _____

Is there a department that can help me develop audiovisual materials for my class?

If yes:
Contact: _____ Phone: _____

Is there an audiovisual library for use by faculty in developing presentation material?

If yes:
Where is it located? _____

Contact: _____ Phone: _____

✔ Where can I obtain the following supplies?

Chalk:

Contact: _____ Phone: _____

Teaching Tools (cont'd)

Whiteboard markers:

    Contact: _____ Phone: _____

Overhead transparency markers:

    Contact: _____ Phone: _____

Overhead transparency film:

    Contact: _____ Phone: _____

Other: _____

    Contact: _____ Phone: _____

✓ Does the school have optical scanning equipment (e.g. Scantron™) to use when grading multiple choice and true/false tests?

    If yes, where is the scanning equipment located?

    _____

    Whom can I ask about how to use the equipment?

    Contact: _____ Phone: _____

    Where can I obtain the mechanical grading forms?

    Contact: _____ Phone: _____

    Where can I obtain pencils for students to use when taking a machine graded test?

    Contact: _____ Phone: _____

NOTES:

_____

_____

_____

_____

_____

Teacher Evaluation

Use the following checklist to make sure you know the steps you have to take to comply with your school's teacher evaluation policy:

✓ When do students complete the teacher evaluations?

_____

✓ What forms are required?

_____

✓ How long does it normally take to administer evaluations?

_____ minutes

✓ What is the procedure for administering the teacher evaluations?

_____

✓ Can I add my own questions to the form (or add a form of my own)?

_____

✓ When do I learn the results of the evaluation?

_____

✓ How is the evaluation used in my performance review?

_____

NOTES:

_____

_____

_____

_____

_____

Administration

Use the following checklist to gather the information you need to meet the administrative and legal requirements of your school:

✓ What employment related forms do I need to fill out?

Form 1: _____

    Contact: _____ Phone: _____

Form 2: _____

    Contact: _____ Phone: _____

✓ What additional information do I need to provide?

    Resume: _____

    College transcripts: _____

    Letters of reference: _____

    Other: _____

    _____

    _____

    _____

    _____

✓ How and when will I be paid?

    _____

Is direct-deposit service available? _____

✓ What services are available to me through the school library?

    _____

    _____

    Contact: _____ Phone: _____

Administration (cont'd)

How can I obtain a library card?

_____

_____

What is the procedure for putting materials on reserve at the library? _____

_____

✓ Is there a computer center or office of computer services that I can call on if I need help?
If yes, where is the office located? _____

_____

Contact: _____ Phone: _____

Is there assistance available in developing classroom materials for use on the computer?

If yes, where is the assistance office located?

_____

Contact: _____ Phone: _____

✓ Where is the closest food service facility/cafeteria to my

classroom? _____

Is there a "faculty" cafeteria?
If yes, where? _____

✓ Are there any additional policies or procedures that I should be aware of? _____

_____

_____

NOTES:

_____

_____

Key Staff

Use the following checklist to recognize key staff at your school and how they can be contacted should the need arise:

✓ Department head/chair, etc.:_____

    Title: _____

    Phone: _____

    Email: _____

✓ Departmental administrative assistant: _____

    Title: _____

    Phone: _____

    Email: _____

✓ Human resources director: _____

    Title: _____

    Phone: _____

    Email: _____

✓ Mentor: _____

    Title: _____

    Phone: _____

    Email: _____

✓ Dean or director of subject area: _____

    Title: _____

    Phone: _____

✓ School president/chancellor: _____

    Administrative assistant: _____

    Phone: _____

Key Staff (cont'd)

✓ Key faculty contact(s):

Contact: _____ Phone: _____

Title: _____

Contact: _____ Phone: _____

Title: _____

Contact: _____ Phone: _____

Title: _____

✓ Campus legal affairs office or ombudsman:

Contact: _____ Phone: _____

✓ Campus police:

Contact: _____ Phone: _____

Campus medical staff:

✓ Contact: _____ Phone: _____

Medical emergency number: _____

✓ Other important contacts:

Contact: _____

Title: _____ Phone: _____

Contact: _____

Title: _____ Phone: _____

Contact: _____

Title: _____ Phone: _____

NOTES:

_____

_____

_____

Chapter 3

Choosing a Textbook

In this chapter:

Is a Textbook Necessary?

No, a textbook isn't necessary, but given the alternatives, you might want to use one. Most alternatives are more time consuming and include:

- Library reading assignments: You will have to review the validity and availability of relevant material in the library before telling your students where to go to find it.

- Books and articles on library reserve: You will need to read, choose, and put books on reserve before the class begins. In addition, you will have to ensure that there are an adequate number of copies on reserve to serve the number of students in your class.

- Photocopied reading packets: These must be approved by the author of the material well in advance of the first class, meet federal copyright laws, and be submitted to the school's copying service (or outside copying service) for duplication prior to your first class.

A L E R T *Advanced Class Materials:* **For some special or advanced classes you may have no choice but to use a collection of articles and book sections because there is no book available that covers the subject adequately.**

For your first class you will probably be better off choosing a textbook as your resource guide rather than developing resources on your own. This is particularly true of survey courses that cover broad subject areas. If you are teaching more specialized subjects you can consider adding more focused material to your course requirements as you get more comfortable with the academic environment you are working in.

In some cases the department chairperson or a departmental committee will have already selected the textbook for your class. Sometimes a specific text will have been selected because it is part of a course series that requires that one text follow another. In some cases you will find that your appointment as a part-time teacher was a last-minute decision and a text has already been chosen so it will be available on the first day of class.

Unfortunately, when new part-time teachers have the option to choose their textbook, many of them allow others to make the choice by default, primarily because they do not understand the textbook selection process, or are afraid of it. Because the textbook is such a critical part of the teaching process, if given the choice, you need to take it upon yourself to choose the best book available.

Textbook Order Status: **Even if the choice of a book has been made by someone else, it's always best to check to see if in fact a book order was placed on your behalf. You never know when an order was misplaced or not filled as required. If there is a problem, see your department head for assistance ASAP.**

How to Get Help in Choosing a Textbook

Ask your department head or another teacher to suggest books they have used in the past. Most full-time teachers receive copies of new or updated editions of textbooks on a regular basis from publishers who want them to adopt their book now or in the future. These are called "desk copies." They will often have a broad selection of these books in the subject area you are interested in. Full-time teachers can also tell you who the area sales representative is for a particular publisher. The school library is another source of textbook choices.

Extra Books: **As a teacher you can also ask publishers for copies of books even if you may not be ready to use them in your next class. There could come a time in the future when you will need another text, and having a copy already in your own personal library will save a lot of time when you have to make a decision. Teachers also use desk copies of other books as reference material when working on lecture notes for their own course. They may find that a particular subject is not adequately covered in the book currently in use and may refer to the material in another book to augment the information.**

The prices of textbooks today will take your breath away. More and more teachers are evaluating the costs of the textbooks and materials their students are having to buy before making a final textbook decision. It's a tough call between product quality and cost. It's important that students get the best book possible, but it's also important that the price is within reason. Try to keep the number of books required to a minimum. That will help.

Trade Press: If you can't find a textbook you like among academic textbook publishers, then you might want to look at the "trade press." These are books that you find in commercial bookstores such as Borders, Barnes and Noble, etc. You may find that even though they are not in an academic format (they often do not have questions at the end of chapters or include case studies, etc.), they can still provide the information you want your students to have. Most can be ordered for use in the classroom by your school's bookstore. Many of the standard textbook publishers have trade press divisions and in many cases can send you desk copies of trade press books through the same system that they would send an academic textbook.

The Textbook Selection Process

Normally the process begins with the bookstore sending a textbook request form to each department head with a due date some months in advance of the term during which the book is to be used. It is then up to each department to gather information on what textbooks need to be ordered. Assuming you have the final responsibility for choosing the textbook, the following people may influence your choice of a textbook:

- Department head
- Curriculum coordinator and other teachers
- Textbook publisher
- Publisher's area "rep"
- School bookstore.

Department head

Your department head may want to review and/or approve the book you have chosen. Make sure you ask what the correct procedure is before going ahead and ordering a book. Department heads will often be more concerned about books that are ordered for required courses than books ordered for elective courses or to meet the needs of more specialized courses.

Curriculum coordinator and other teachers

Your schools curriculum coordinator or other teachers may have already specified a textbook that fits into a specific set of courses or one that meets the needs of a curriculum coordinating body at your school.

Textbook publisher

Dealing with textbook publishers is an art. There are few up-to-date directories of publishers, and the contact names change frequently. This situation is aggravated by the consolidation going on in the textbook industry today. A good place to start is your school bookstore. They can tell you who their current contacts are for purchasing textbooks.

In many school bookstores you will find a thick reference book called "Book Buyer's Manual." It's published by the National Association of College Stores (NACS) and is a directory of publishers, distributors, and wholesalers serving college and university bookstores. It's the textbook industry's reference resource for institutions of higher learning. You can visit the NACS Web site at www.nacs.org for more information.

So, once you have the names of publishers, what do you want to find out when you contact them? For starters:

- Find out what books they currently have available in your subject area and what edition they are.
- Find out when a new addition of a current book is planned.

- Find out how to order a copy of the book(s) you are interested in reviewing. Although it will depend to some extent on the size of your school and the potential sales for the book publisher, in most cases the copy will be free.

- Find out the name of the area representative who handles their line of books in your area.

Several tools (desk copies, instructor's guides, computer generated test banks, etc.) are available free-of-charge to the teacher adopting a textbook. It is best if you contact the publisher or publisher's representative directly and ask for these items. At the very least the publisher should provide free-of-charge an instructor's copy of the textbook and an instructor's manual/resource guide, whether you adopt it or not. Remember, publishers want you to order their book, and you can't do that if you haven't evaluated the book or some of the support materials that come with it.

Ordering Desk Copies: **In most cases publishers will only send a desk copy to your attention at the school at which you will be teaching, not to your home. This is to ensure that you are a bona fide teacher at a particular institution. Make sure when ordering a desk copy that you have the exact address of your department and school ready at hand when placing the order. And make sure the mailroom at your school knows who you are! You may also want to alert someone in the departmental office that material will be coming in under your name.**

Publisher's area "rep"

Area representatives often work out of their homes and cover a large territory. You should develop a relationship with your publisher's rep, even if it is only by phone. They can tell you when new editions are coming out and what new support materials are available for a particular book. They can also expedite shipments and troubleshoot for you if necessary when a particular book is out-of-stock or late in arriving.

School bookstore

Although students often complain about them, bookstores are a critical part of the academic system for both teachers and students. Bookstores collect book orders, order and stock books, price books, help teachers connect with textbook publishers, and provide a whole host of other services that take place behind the scenes. Given all the tasks that bookstore staff carry out on a daily basis, it's important that you provide them with as much information as you can on the book or book "package" that you want them to make available to your students. The following information should be given to the bookstore, usually via a textbook request form:

1. Textbook title
2. Textbook author
3. Textbook publisher
4. Copyright date
5. Edition
6. ISBN number
7. Order quantity.

Textbooks On-line: **The Internet is shaking up the college bookstore system as it is all other facets of academic life. Web sites like www.varsitybooks.com and www. amazon.com offer textbooks at significant discounts over college bookstore prices.**

The Importance of ISBN Numbers: **Every book now in print has an International Standard Book Number (ISBN), often found on the copyright page of each book. This comes in handy when ordering the right book for your class. For instance, different editions of the same book will have different ISBN numbers. In some cases publishers assign special ISBN numbers to "packages" which might include a book (having one ISBN number) and a student workbook (having a different ISBN number). Providing the correct ISBN number with your order ensures that the bookstore orders the right book or package.**

Making the Final Choice

One way to make sure you choose the right book is to find several textbooks that address the subject area you will be teaching. Then, review the chapter headings and subheadings in the front of the book. And finally, carefully read the first two or three chapters of each book, noting the following as you read along:

- Does it flow well; are concepts laid out in a well-thought-out way?

- Is it presented in a logical, structured manner?

- Are you comfortable with the level of difficulty of the material?

- Does the book have the tools you need, for example, questions at the end of the chapters, cases, etc.?

- Is the book consistent throughout?

- Is the book too long for the amount of time given to teach the material in it? Too short?

- Do you like the book (a very subjective, but important element in the equation)? That is, do you feel it presents the subject matter in a way that is consistent with your own understanding of the subject?

Choosing a textbook can be pretty intimidating for the uninitiated. As mentioned earlier, new part-time teachers do not always have the authority to choose their own book. Or, they will be able to choose only books that meet a minimum number of school requirements. Yet, should you be allowed to choose your own book, following are some tips to make the process a little more manageable.

Choose textbooks on the following criteria:

Content: You want to choose a book you can understand. This might be self-evident, but to the new part-time teacher it can be critical. Why? Because many part-time teachers hold professional positions outside of academia, and although they have the work experience in a particular subject area, they are not always up on the theoretical side of the subject or on the more advanced work being done in the field. In addition, part-time professors will often find themselves looking at a term or concept in a book and thinking to themselves, "Is that what that's called?" They know the subject from experience, but not what its formal definition is.

In many cases teachers will have to learn a whole new way of saying things that for years they just took for granted or used different terms to describe. The clearer the book is to you, the clearer it will be to your students. This is also why it's good to review several texts to get as much information as possible about a subject. And, it's important that you review the material far enough ahead of time to be able to absorb the new terms and concepts and incorporate them into your real-world experiences. It also helps if you develop an outline of the chapters before you begin teaching to give you an idea of the structure of the material and how best to incorporate it into your class discussions.

Many part-time teachers will, by nature, gravitate to the more "applied" style of textbook, rather than one that is more theoretical in nature. Many schools hire part-time teachers for their applied view of the world. But don't exclude a textbook from consideration just because it delves more into the theoretical side of a subject than you would like. Students need to have a well-rounded view of your subject, and that includes the theoretical as well as the practical. Ask other professors in your discipline (whether at your school or at other schools in the area) what they think the pros and cons of a particular book are. And then make your choice.

Clarity: The material should be clear and concise with enough explanation to make the subject matter understandable, yet not so detailed that it overwhelms the student. You might ask the chairperson or others who have taught your course in the past what they feel is the level of understanding of the particular class you will be teaching (freshmen, senior, graduate, etc.). Being able to judge what is too little or too much will take some time and experience on your part, so don't feel bad if you don't get it right the first (or second) time.

Ease of use: A text should be laid out in a logical manner with simple textual aids to help with understanding and organization. Many books are now formatted so that the left margin of each page provides an outline or brief review of what is found in the corresponding paragraph or section. You can use these reviews to key into your discussion notes. If you have the time, do a quick outline of one or two chapters of each of the books you have chosen to review. In this way you will soon get a feeling for how a book flows and how your lectures and discussions would flow using it.

 Book Length: **Another key for ease-of-use is that you can cover the material in the book in the time allotted for the course. Here length and complexity play a big part in which book is most appropriate.**

Support material: Textbook publishers provide a number of support tools to make your job easier when choosing and using their books:

1. Instructor's manuals or resource guides that can include:
   - lecture outlines
   - study questions
   - test questions
   - black-and-white printed copies of overheads
   - material that supports subjects covered in the text
   - chapter-by-chapter discussions of the material
   - case studies
   - supplementary reading lists
   - suggested course outlines

2. Computerized test banks (floppy disk or CD)

3. Transparencies/overheads/acetates for use in classroom

4. Video libraries

5. Computer presentations (for example, PowerPoint® slides) covering coursework

6. Maps.

A L E R T

Get the Latest Edition: **Make sure you are evaluating the latest edition of the book you have chosen to review. Nothing is more frustrating than to find you've reviewed and perhaps outlined sections of a book that is no longer in print or soon to go out of print.**

The "author-ity" question

Often new teachers assume that because "Dr. So-and-so" wrote a book" it must be a well-written book that students will find easy to understand. Unfortunately, just because a professor writes a book does not mean that it is a well-written textbook. There are both very good and very poor textbooks on the market today. It's your job to separate the good from the bad – no one else's.

Changing a Textbook – Pain vs. Gain

Two challenges face teachers who want to change textbooks. One is the problem facing teachers when changing textbooks too often, and the other is not changing textbooks often enough.

There is a common tendency for teachers who have put many hours into lecture development and outlines to resist changing books because of the time required to update and revise lecture notes. This is particularly true for teachers who don't have the time to revise their lecture notes on a regular basis. However, depending on the subject matter, textbooks can become quickly outdated. For instance, a book on international business can become outdated as quickly as the global picture changes. Yet, a text on 19th-century American literature is seldom outdated in the same sense. Be careful that you do not continue to use a book too long after more current and more helpful books have become available.

Of course the flip side of this is changing texts too often. Going from one text to another can be an incredibly time consuming and nerve wracking experience. Every author has his or her own style and idea of what is important to emphasize in a course. Revising notes and lecture materials to meet a new author's format can be a nightmare, not only in the time it takes to revise notes, but also the time it may take to learn new concepts and terms. Make sure your reasons for changing books (and publishers) are valid.

The Consequences of Dropping Textbooks: **Students often sell textbooks back to the bookstore at the end of the term for resale as used textbooks the next time the course is taught. They will receive a larger refund if the same book is going to be used again than if you are going to use another book. If that particular edition is going out of print, they will receive even less, or nothing at all.**

Changing Textbooks: **If you do plan to change your textbook, do it over the summer when you have more time. Changing a textbook between terms only compounds the work involved in updating your notes, revising overheads, etc. Be careful when switching textbooks from one term to another that you don't assume your class is reading something that was actually in the previous textbook, not the current one. Always check to see that key concepts in your lecture notes are explained in the new text.**

Monitoring Textbook Delivery: **Bookstore personnel have a lot to do, and sometimes book orders get lost or are delayed through no fault of the bookstore. You need to monitor the stocking status of your book to ensure that when students come to your first class they do so with the right book(s) in hand. If you can't go to the bookstore before class starts, call the textbook manager at the bookstore directly. A missing textbook can mean ruined schedules and hours spent in front of a copying machine generating the materials your students will have to use until the right book(s) arrives.**

Your Bookstore Contact: **Get to know the textbook manager at your bookstore, even if only by phone. He or she is a key person in the book ordering process, and you never know when you will have to call upon someone in an emergency.**

Chapter 4

Developing Your Syllabus

In this chapter:

It's a Contract!

The syllabus is one of the most important documents in your portfolio of teaching tools and often the most neglected. A detailed syllabus minimizes the amount of time that a teacher has to spend outside of class explaining class structure and course requirements. The syllabus is where you clearly explain what you plan to accomplish in the class, what the timetable is for accomplishing those tasks, what is expected of the students, and how the students will be evaluated on their progress. In essence, the syllabus is a "performance contract" between you and your students. If all of the major points are covered in the syllabus, miscommunication and misunderstanding are kept to an absolute minimum. From the viewpoint of students this is particularly critical since part-time teachers are often difficult to contact outside of office hours.

This is one of the longest chapters in this manual. We wanted to include everything you will need to prepare your own syllabus. Below is an example of what your completed syllabus might look like.

Modern European History
HS 4215-002 Fall Term, 2000
Monday: 6:00 — 8:50 PM

Instructor:	Mr. John McGuire
Office:	Cramer Bldg., Room 107
Office Hours:	Monday by appointment
Telephone:	School: (542) 255-8900 (Mrs. Malloy)
Email:	jmcguire@ccl.net
Textbook:	The History of Modern Europe (second edition), C.L. White, State University Press, 2000.

Purpose of Course: The purpose of this course is to have the student critically evaluate the history of Europe from 1870 to the present day.

Objectives:
1. Introduce the student to the major historical figures of the time period
2. Help the student understand the societal pressures of the era
3. Help the student understand the economic policies that helped mold the historical developments of this critical period in history
4. Help the student understand the critical role Europe will play in the next century.

Methodology: During each class we will discuss the material in the assigned chapter. You will be responsible for having read the material prior to class and be ready to participate in the class discussions. A significant portion of your final grade will depend on your participation in class discussions, as they will focus on helping you understand how the different periods of modern European history are interrelated.

A group project is due the week before the final exam. The timetable for organizing your work and completing the project on time is in the course outline that follows. During the second week of class you will be given an information sheet that outlines the goals and structure of the project as well as your team assignments. If you have any questions about the assignments or your role as team member after we have reviewed the information in class, contact the instructor.

Evaluation: In addition to the project, there will be a final exam at the end of the term as well as a mid-term exam and three unannounced quizzes. The grading system is as follows:

		Points	Grading Scale
1.	Class participation	100	608 - 675 = A
2.	Quizzes (25 pts. Each)	75	540 - 607 = B
3.	Mid-term exam	100	473 - 539 = C
4.	Project	200	405 - 472 = D
5.	Final exam	200	Below 405 = F
	TOTAL	675	

Note 1: Attendance will be taken at the beginning of each class.

Note 2: There will be no make-ups possible on the quizzes. Make-ups on exams will be considered on a case-by-case basis.

Course Outline

DATE	TOPIC	CH.	ASSIGNMENTS
M - 9/11	Prewar Europe	1	-------
M - 9/18	World War I	2	Answer questions pg. 96
			Turn in project topic
M - 9/25	Europe 1919 - 1929	3	Review questions pg. 134
			(be ready to discuss)
M - 10/2	Europe 1929 - 1939	4	Project update due (1 pg.)
	NOTE: 10/2 is last date to withdraw from class		
M - 10/9	MID-TERM EXAM	-	-
M - 10/16	TERM BREAK	-	-
M - 10/23	World War II	5	Answer questions pg. 230
M - 10/30	Postwar Europe	6	Project: Present phase I
M - 11/6	Postwar Europe	7	Answer questions pg. 330
M - 11/13	Europe in Transition	8	Review questions pg. 367
M - 11/20	HOLIDAY BREAK	-	-
M - 11/27	Project presentations	-	-
M - 12/4	Review for final	1 - 8	Bring questions
M - 12/11	FINAL EXAM	6:00 PM to 9:00 PM	

M = Monday

Using the Syllabus

Make sure that you go over your syllabus thoroughly during the first or second class period to make sure all your students understand what is expected of them. If students see that you consider the syllabus an important document, they will also consider it important. Have it with you at all times so when a student asks a question that can be answered by referring to the syllabus, you can get to it quickly.

Many professors now put their syllabi on their school's Web server so students can access the information and print it off prior to the first class. As a part-time professor you may or may not have the time or the expertise to do this for your students. Ask your supervisor if your school provides assistance in this area.

Information, Please!

The first section of your syllabus should provide the following course information:

1. Course title

2. Course number (and section number if applicable)

3. Term taught

4. Time class meets

Your Credentials

The next section should provide information about you that includes:

1. Name (as you want your students to address you, for example, Mr. Smith or John Smith)

2. Your academic or professional title, for example, Ph.D., M.S., M.B.A., C.P.A., etc. (check departmental practice)

3. Office, room number (if applicable)

4. Office hours

5. Office phone, fax, email, etc. (if applicable)

6. Personal phone, fax, email (optional).

Your Office: **As a part-time instructor you will probably not have the luxury of an office of your own. Some schools provide an office that all part-time and adjunct faculty share when on campus. Other schools provide no facilities at all. If you do not have the use of office space, you may want to ask the school to designate a place where you can meet with students before class or at other times when they need help (e.g. in an empty classroom, the department conference room, a study room in the library, etc.). If your classroom is available before or after class you can meet students there. As a last resort you can decide on a central meeting point on campus where you can meet a student and then go somewhere else to sit down and talk. If you decide to use this method make sure you indicate the meeting point on your syllabus.**

Mailboxes: **Most schools provide part-time instructors with a mail box in the department office. Make sure you let your students know that they can always leave non-urgent materials there for you to pick up when you come in to teach. If you know how often you will be checking for mail, let them know that, too.**

Telephone Number: **If the telephone number provided in the syllabus is that of the department secretary or other departmental staff, note it next to the phone number, and if possible, provide that person's name (after having first asked permission from that person). The same holds true for departmental email addresses.**

Prerequisites: **The prerequisite classes students need to have to take your course (for example, a student is to have taken History 2500 before they can take History 4215) should have been addressed when the student signed up for your course. But, if you wish to avoid any misunderstandings, you can include this requirement in your syllabus.**

Telephone Limits: **If you put your home phone number in the syllabus and do not want to be called at all hours of the day or night, designate a time limit like, "No calls after 8:00 p.m., please."**

Many part-time instructors do not have the time to set aside an hour or so before or after each class to wait for students to come in and discuss problems they may be having. In this case it is better to say in the syllabus, "Office hours by appointment only." Yet, you need to make it clear during the first class that you are interested in seeing any student who is having a problem, and you are more than happy to set up a time to meet if they call you for an appointment in advance. You might want to tell your students you are willing to meet with them before class if they call you in advance. Another option is to say you will stay after class if a student lets you know before the class starts that he or she wants to talk to you.

Course Materials

You should include <u>all</u> the materials required to complete your course.

The textbook

The textbook is the foundation upon which most courses are built. The key information you will need to give your students concerning the textbook is:

1. Title

2. Edition

3. Author(s)

4. Publisher

5. Publication date

6. ISBN (International Standard Book Number) number

7. Where textbook can be purchased (optional), e.g. college bookstore, retail bookstore, etc. This information is more relevant for part-time and non-traditional students who may be unfamiliar with where they can purchase materials.

You will find more help on actually choosing a textbook back in Chapter 3.

You should read your textbook from cover to cover. If you only have time to read through the textbook once, make sure your first reading is a thorough one. Having your students point out key concepts in the text that you missed is not a good way to win your school's teacher of the year award. So, take your time going through the textbook and make notes to use in your presentation as you read through it. Also, look through any teaching manuals, test banks, PowerPoint presentations, etc. that come with the book to learn what is available to you as you develop your course. Review the section on chapter outlines in Chapter 7 for help in organizing your thoughts as you read through the textbook.

No Books! Be prepared to find students in your first class who have not yet purchased the textbook or other required course materials. Some students will be deciding first if they want to continue with the class or drop it. Other students will be trying to determine if they can get by without having to buy the book by borrowing another student's book or by copying parts of another student's book. Some will be trying to determine if the teacher gives out all the necessary information during class (in lectures), therefore making the book redundant. Some non-traditional students just may not have had the time before the first class to go to the campus bookstore and buy the book.

Syllabus Wording re Text: To avoid any confusion in the syllabus as to what is required and what is not, you might want to use the phrase "Required Text" in your syllabus rather than just "Textbook" or "Text." If you want to suggest books or articles that the students might want to read to supplement the information in the text, but that are not needed to meet the requirements of the course, you can provide an additional category called "Suggested Reading."

Articles

When choosing articles for your students to read, you should include in the syllabus the following information:

1. Title of article
2. Publication article can be found in
3. Date of publication
4. Volume number of publication (if applicable)
5. Page number(s) of article (beginning and end)
6. Where article or copy of article is available (library reserve, bookstore, copy center, etc.).

Other materials

When choosing other course material (e.g. art supplies, engineering supplies, scientific equipment, etc.) it's important to include the following in your syllabus:

1. Spell out exactly how, when, and where materials can be obtained

2. Indicate any safety issues that need to be considered when buying any equipment, chemicals, etc.

 Know the Price: Even though you don't have to put the price of the book or materials in the syllabus, it's always good to know prices should students bring up the subject in class. Textbook prices have risen significantly in the last ten years, and if you know the price of the text being used it shows the students you care enough to know what they have to shell out, even if it seems high.

Goals and Purpose

Course purpose

The course purpose section briefly lays out for students your overall goal for the course. It should state in one or two sentences what the students should be thinking, doing, or saying as a result of having taken your course. The information in the course objectives (below) will provide the detail. You may want to combine this section with the objectives and put it all under a single heading, "Course Description."

Course objectives

Course objectives should provide a more detailed description of how the purpose of the course (or goal) is to be accomplished. The course objectives can be stated in a simple one-or two-paragraph description of what students should come away with from the course, or they can be included in a more structured description of the course with objectives laid out in bulleted form.

Informational versus outcome objectives:

Many teachers think that "information" is what their students should know when the term is over and that information and "course objectives" are one and the same. Yet, if teachers want to develop course objectives that really mean something to their students – course objectives that will have a real impact on their students' lives once they are out in the world – teachers need to develop course objectives from a different perspective. They need to ask themselves not what information they want their students to know at the end of the term, but what they want their students to be doing, thinking, or saying as a result of having taken their course.

For example, take the following course objective for a typical marketing course:

> *Students should be able to describe the four P's of marketing (product, price, promotion, place).*

This objective asks that the student be able to recite from memory specific information that will be presented during the term. This is an example of an "informational objective."

Now let's develop a course objective that focuses on outcome rather than means. By focussing on "outcome objectives," teachers compel students to develop their higher level intellectual skills.

> *Using the four P's of marketing as a basis, students will be able to analyze everyday marketing practices and link this analysis to real-world business situations.*

In the example above, if the course is successful, students will leave it with valuable analytical skills they can use in the world of business management.

If we take the informational objectives from the syllabus you saw at the beginning of this chapter and turn them into outcome objectives, they might read as follows:

---

1. *Students will be able to relate how the major historical figures of the time affected the period they lived in and how their actions affected the future of Europe, as well.*
2. *Students will be able to isolate the societal pressures in each era and show how they contributed to the flow of history from that point forward.*
3. *Students will be able to analyze the economic policies that helped mold the historical events of each period and use this analysis to interpret current events taking place in the area.*
4. *Students will be able to describe to others outside of the classroom the critical role Europe will play in the new century.*

Using outcome objectives? Outcome objectives are

not as easy to develop as are informational objectives. The skill needed to develop effective outcome objectives often comes with experience in using them. Both full- and part-time teachers have a hard time setting aside the extra time it takes to generate, plan for and teach a course that uses outcome objectives as its focus. Teachers using outcome objectives also have to make sure their teaching style supports the discussion and analysis that outcome objectives require. Yet the results of using outcome objectives are clearly superior to those accomplished using informational objectives.

Many teachers start out with informational objectives and move to outcome objectives as they gain experience in generating more meaningful, reality-based objectives. The quicker you can move from informational to outcome objectives in your class, the quicker your students will benefit from this more effective approach.

If you are not sure what the course objectives should be, talk to your department head, mentor or another teacher to get a feeling for what might be a good direction for you to take. In some schools, certain departments may have set objectives for each course that you need to follow, particularly if the course is part of a series of courses that students must take to complete a major or minor requirement. You may want to use the course description found in your school's course catalog as a starting point for developing your own objectives.

Reviewing course objectives

For the most part, course objectives are on the syllabus for your use during the first day of class to help point out to your students what they should focus on as they move through the course material. It's also a way for you to let the class know some of the activities that are going to take place over the term that will help them acquire the skills you have outlined in the course description. Realistically speaking, having reviewed this once in class, your students will probably never look at the objectives again. So, make the most of it while you have their attention.

Drop and Add Decisions: **Some students use the course description to determine whether they drop the course or stay with it. If after having read your course description students drop your course and sign up for another, don't take it personally. This is part of the normal decision making process in schools today.**

Course Description

Use the following form to build your course description. It will change over time, so don't worry about being perfect the first time out. Just getting your thoughts down on paper will help you as your teaching plan develops.

✔ Course name: _____

✔ Course purpose:_____

       _____

       _____

Course Description (cont'd)

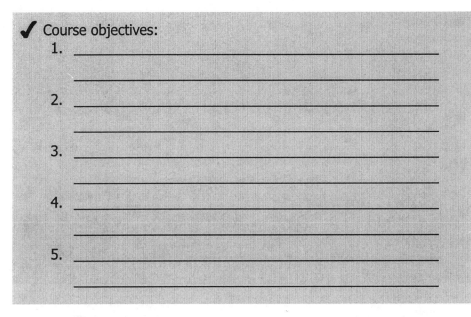

✔ Course objectives:
1. _____
   _____
2. _____
   _____
3. _____
   _____
4. _____
   _____
5. _____
   _____

Methodology

This section of the syllabus should include a review of the activities that make up the cooperative learning experience between students and teacher. This section describes presentation and discussion ground rules, outside reading requirements, projects, case assignments, homework assignments, and exams that make up the course. Each activity should be explained in detail so students can get answers to most of their course content questions by going to the relevant section of the syllabus. It's better to err on the side of too much information, rather than too little.

Evaluation

This section of the syllabus describes how students are to be evaluated during the term and how their final grades are to be determined. It should include a description of all the evaluation tools (quizzes, exams, homework) to be used during the course of the school term. It should also provide a description of how the other activities listed in the methodology section (for example projects or class participation) will be used to evaluate the student's performance. Make sure to ask your department head if there are any departmental or school-wide grading policies or rules-of-thumb that have to be taken into consideration when coming up with a grading policy of your own.

Your attendance policy can be stated in this section or in a separate section if you want to emphasize the importance of good attendance.

Use of Due Dates: **To minimize confusion, make sure you list project due dates in the course outline/assignments section of your syllabus. It's also a good place to state your policies on accepting work late (e.g. whether you permit students to take exams they missed and how you grade late exams).**

What's an "A"? **Make sure you explain your grading criteria to your students. Show them what "A" work looks like, what criteria it meets. Hand out an old test or quiz, or make up a sample test and give it to your students so they can see the type and style of questions you expect them to respond to.**

For more information on grading, turn to Part IV, "Evaluating Students."

Attendance

Make sure you spell out in detail your attendance policy and how students will be evaluated on attendance. Clearly state which absences are excused and which are not. If the only legitimate excuse in your mind is a student's own demise, then make sure students know it.

Stressing Attendance: **No matter your reasons for wanting students to attend class, emphasize during the syllabus review session the importance of good attendance. You might want to point out that additional material will be provided in class, that in-depth analysis of pertinent topics will be done in class, or that you will be grading students on class participation during the class discussion times.**

Course Outline: Schedule and Assignments

This is a list of the class assignments with appropriate dates and responsibilities. Students consider this the most important part of the syllabus. Make sure you clearly spell out in the outline what is expected of each student over the school term. Do not hesitate to add a page or two if needed. Too much information is always better than too little when outlining assignments. Refer back to the syllabus at the beginning of this chapter for an example of how a course outline might look.

 Course Outline Detail: **When assigning due dates, include in your course outline exams, holidays, school vacation days, etc. This will ensure that both you and the students have a clear picture of the time available. It will also give you a better sense of how the course will actually unfold during the term.**

 Put Most Important Up Front: **You may find it to your advantage to make the course assignment page the first page of your syllabus. This will be the page you and your students refer to most during the term, and it should be readily available. All the rest of the information included in the syllabus is really the detail that supports the course assignment schedule. To make the course assignment page the first one, use a header with course, title, section number, term, and your name across the top. Then follow this with the course assignments. Then complete the syllabus with the remainder of the information as discussed in this chapter.**

How much time does it take?

The first question many new teachers ask is, "How much class time do I need to plan for when laying out the course assignment page of the syllabus?" The answer will depend on the subject being taught, the number of students in the class, and the different types of learning tools used (lectures, discussions, cases, projects, etc.). As you become more experienced, you will get a better feel for how much material is normally covered in a typical class period. To help you keep track of the amount of time it takes to cover a particular subject, or to use a particular evaluation tool (exam, quiz, etc.), it's best to keep a log of how long these tasks have taken in the past. You might want to develop a log, like the one shown in the example that follows, to record the amount of time needed to cover individual activities in your class. Particularly when starting out in teaching, you need to record this data before you forget it. This time sheet will come in very handy when planning future classes. You can also get an idea from other teachers in your subject area as to how much time you should set aside to cover a particular subject or complete a particular activity.

Time Record

Use the following chart to record the time spent on various activities that take place during your class. Record the time over several school terms (#1, #2, #3) to get a consistent reading. Use these time intervals to help plan future classes.

Activity	Time Required in Minutes		
	#1	#2	#3
✓ Taking attendance			
✓ Chapter discussion			
✓ Giving a quiz			
✓ Giving an exam			
✓ Discussing an exam			
✓ Other:			
✓ Other:			
✓ Other:			
✓ Other:			

Schools often break up "three credit hour" classes into one-hour sessions (class meets three times a week), hour-and-a-half sessions (class meets twice a week), or three-hour sessions (class meets once a week). Remember that this block of time often includes a 10- to 15-minute break between classes as well as any additional breaks you might add (for example, a break halfway through a three-hour class). When planning for a class, teachers need to take into account the time lost on administrative duties like taking attendance and handing back graded assignments when each class begins. For example, in many schools a one-hour class is actually 50 minutes long because of the break between classes. Add to this the time spent on administrative duties, say five minutes, and you have a class of only 45 minutes. As the class length increases, the impact of time lost to administrative duties per minutes of actual class time available decreases. For this reason, you will probably find you can cover more material in a class that meets twice a week than one that meets three times a week.

Other Information

School Policy: Do's and Don'ts

Each school has its own policies concerning classroom behavior such as absences or cheating on tests. Those that directly affect your class and the ability of your students to meet class requirements should be included in the syllabus. Academic integrity codes can usually be found in the school catalog and copied directly into the syllabus.

Again, it is always best to err on the side of too much information in your syllabus, rather than too little. For example, if there are safety issues concerning equipment or materials used in a particular class, this should be clearly explained in the syllabus.

Technology Considerations

Some colleges and universities are responding to the rapid growth in computer technology by upgrading classrooms, libraries, and living areas with the latest in communication technology. Other schools, because of budget and/or manpower constraints, are just beginning to respond to the need. You need to find out what the available level of technology is in your school and what the basic communication technology tools you are expected to use are.

Revising the Contract

A syllabus is a work-in-progress. Each class term you will find yourself revising the last version to make it a better teaching tool. Because a syllabus has to meet the needs of an ever-changing population of students, you'll need to build some flexibility into it. Make sure you build some extra time into your class schedule for unexpected delays. For example, you should always build in the time it will take students to full out the teacher evaluations at the end of the term. If you find that a particular teaching tool is not working as expected, be ready to discard it and move on to something else. Don't waste your time and that of your students trying to adhere to the schedule in your syllabus when you know it is no longer realistic.

On the other hand, you need to make decisions regarding mid-term changes to your syllabus with care. Students look to the syllabus as their point of reference for all activities that concern your course, and veering from its schedule and tools too often will give the students the impression you are "making it up as you do along."

 Testing Your Syllabus: **Ask former students or current students not taking your course to review your syllabus before you hand it out. They can often spot those areas of the syllabus that are unclear or need more explanation.**

NOTES:

_____

_____

_____

Chapter 5

Using Classroom Tools

In this chapter:

Plan First!

There are a number of tools that can help you be a better teacher. Suffice it to say that you need to plan how and when you use these tools. And you need to ensure that each tool you use contributes positively to the overall effectiveness of your classroom activities. Otherwise, it is a waste of your (and your students') time. Some of the information gathered using the checklists in Chapter 2 will help you with this planning task.

Overheads

There are three ways you can use overhead transparencies in the classroom. One is by using the transparencies that textbook publishers often include with their textbooks. A second way is by first developing a concept on paper and then transferring it to the transparency using a photocopier or transparency copier. The third way is by using a blank transparency (rather than the blackboard) to write down concepts freehand before class or as you move through the material in the classroom. All three require that you use a transparency projector or other electronic imaging equipment to display the material in the classroom.

When making your own overhead transparencies you should limit the information on each transparency to one central idea. You can usually accomplish this by providing the information using three to five points per page. In addition, it's better to use several simple transparencies rather than a single complicated one to explain a concept or idea. When transferring copy to an overhead transparency make sure the copy is large enough that the students in the back of the room can see it. Letters should usually be a minimum of 1/4" to 3/8" high (font size of 18 point or higher). Use a template the size of your projector's viewing surface to ensure that the material will fit within the projection area.

Overhead Content: **Experiment with the amount of information you can put on each overhead and still have it be readable. This includes experimenting with text point size (e.g. 18, 22, 26, 32, etc.) to determine what works best in your classroom.**

Equipment and classroom check-up

Try to review equipment placement and lighting before the term begins to ensure that it is ready for your use. You should consider the following:

Projector Availability: Find out if all classrooms are equipped with an overhead projector or piece of electronic imaging equipment, or whether you have to order the equipment for each class period in which you want to use it. Your classroom may be equipped with one of the following:

- A standard overhead projector that transfers an image on a transparency via a mirror to the projection screen

- Electronic imaging equipment connected to a TV monitor or multimedia projector

- A computer connected to a TV monitor or multimedia projector.

Electronic Imaging Equipment: Electronic imaging equipment usually consists of a base on which you can lay overheads, other two-dimensional pictures, or three-dimensional objects. Above the base are light sources and a camera head. In the overhead mode the equipment functions like a standard overhead projector, the only difference being that the visual image is projected onto a screen or TV monitor via a camera and an electronic projection unit rather than via the light and mirror system of a conventional overhead projector. In the visual presentation mode the overhead camera picks up the image of picture or text on a piece of paper, or the actual image of a three-dimensional object, and projects it onto the screen or monitor using an electronic projector. You will need to plan for using pictures and text on paper as well as three-dimensional objects if you decide to use this equipment. You will also have to decide how best to bring the materials into the classroom. Questions you need to ask yourself are:

- Do you know how to use the projection equipment?

- Will the three-dimensional objects fit into your briefcase?

- Do you want the class to see the pictures or objects before you are ready to present them? If not, how are you going to keep them out of sight until the right moment?

- Does your projector provide enough detail of the three-dimensional objects to be seen clearly on the screen in front of the classroom?

Lighting: Find out what the lighting conditions are in your classroom. Do most of the lights have to be turned off to read the material on the screen? If so, it makes it harder for students to take notes. Find out which light switches have to be shut off so you don't have to waste time testing each one in class to get the best lighting effect. Classrooms equipped with dimmer switches will make your job easier.

Making Overheads: Find out where you have to go to make overheads. Also, find out where the supply of blank overhead film is located. There are three methods commonly used today to produce transparencies from printed material.

Photocopier generated: A transparency is placed in a photocopier's paper tray just as a regular piece of paper would be.

Thermal copier generated: Thermal copies are made by transferring the image from the original document to a thin piece of film using heat to set the image on the film. It is a quick and easy way to make overheads and is significantly cheaper than using photocopier film. The drawbacks are that the transparency must be handled carefully because the thermal transparency film is much thinner than standard photocopier film. Thermal copies can also darken with age, particularly when exposed to light.

Laser printer/computer generated: Transparency film is placed in the paper tray of a laser printer and a print made on the film of the image on the computer monitor.

Equipment Placement: Decide where you will locate the projection equipment in the classroom. And then ask yourself the following questions. Will it block your interaction with your students? Is it too heavy to lift up and down easily should you want to remove it when not in use? Can it be moved at all? Is it far away enough from the screen that the picture is big enough to see even in the back of the classroom? Is there an electrical outlet nearby, or will you need an extension cord?

Supplies: Find out where you can obtain the necessary supplies to use, clean, and maintain overheads when you use them in class.

Felt-tip markers: Both water-soluble and permanent markers are available. If you want to be able to modify information, use the water-soluble type. When using water-soluble markers make sure you have an absorbent cloth and a water source available (such as a spray bottle) for cleaning the transparency film. When printing on film, the letters should be a ¼" high or higher, and you should use black, green, brown, or blue felt-tip markers whenever possible. Colors like orange, red, or yellow are hard to see from a distance.

Spare bulbs: Do you know where the spare projector bulbs are located? Can you switch bulbs mechanically without having to open up the projector? How does the bulb switching mechanism work?

 File Those Transparencies: **Transparencies are easily mixed up or misplaced if not stored in an easy-to-use file. You can use clear plastic sleeves to hold overhead transparencies and place them on the projector still in the sleeve.**

 Hole Punching Transparencies: **If you want to punch holes in a transparency for storage in a 3-ring binder, be careful that your punch is sharp. You can prevent transparencies from jamming in the punch by putting several sheets of scrap paper on either side of the transparency before punching.**

Running "Test" Copies: **Transparency film for use in photocopiers and laser printers is expensive. Make sure the material you want copied is correct before transferring it to copier transparency film. Always run a regular photocopy to check placement and contrast. Then put the overhead film in the same paper tray and hit the copy button.**

Videos

Showing videos offers both opportunities and challenges. As with all equipment use, you will need to determine beforehand whether your classroom has video equipment installed or whether you have to order it. You will also need to decide whether there is enough time to show the video material – which you have to review carefully before showing it – and still cover the other material you want to cover in class. Remember to include in your planning the time it takes to turn on the monitor, load the cassette, and adjust the sound.

Video Formats: If you happen to see a video you are interested in purchasing that was produced outside the United States, make sure it is available in the U.S. video format (NTSC) before ordering it, or it may not work on the video equipment in your classroom. Formats commonly used outside the U.S. are PAL and SECAM.

Blackboards and Whiteboards

If used correctly, blackboards and whiteboards can be effective teaching tools. If used incorrectly they can lead to confusion and misunderstanding. Before your first class make sure the classroom assigned to you has either a blackboard (often green in color, although they are still referred to as blackboards) or whiteboard and that you have the supplies to use them (chalk or markers and erasers).

Take Extra Supplies: **Make sure you carry extra chalk or whiteboard markers with you to class. You never know when the classroom supplies might be missing.**

Blackboard Magnets: **Today's blackboards are often made of a thin piece of flat steel covered with a special surface material. Buy a packet of small magnets to post up maps, discussion photos, etc.**

> **T**
> **I**
> **P**
>
> *Erase That Board!:* **It is common courtesy to clean the board(s) after each class in preparation for the next class to use that room.**

Slides

Slides can be used to highlight important concepts, but have several drawbacks and are not often used in today's classrooms:

- Slides have to be developed before class

- The use of slides requires that all lights (or most) be turned out

- Slides require special projectors and control equipment.

Computers

Many of today's classrooms are equipped with computers and the equipment to project a computer image onto a screen in front of the class. With the availability of software programs like PowerPoint, teachers can project sophisticated, easily updated images onto the screen. A whole host of images can be easily downloaded from the Internet and presented through the computer interface. To be an effective teacher using this medium, you must know the equipment and how to use it. Test the equipment in advance of class time to ensure that your software is compatible with the equipment in the classroom. And always have backup material on overheads in case the computer goes down.

> **A**
> **L**
> **E**
> **R**
> **T**
>
> *Scheduling Equipment:* **In some cases, the classroom equipment will already have been scheduled for part-time teachers before they begin the term. But, it's always best to double check with the department head or secretary to ensure that the required scheduling has been done before classes start.**

Handouts and Books on Reserve

Some teachers assign too much outside reading material. Others don't provide adequate guidelines on how to work effectively through the readings they do assign. Some teachers assume students can assimilate the material as fast as the teacher can, and at the same interest level. To avoid these pitfalls the teacher must critically review each handout before the class to ensure that the material meets the needs of the teacher <u>and</u> the students and that adequate time is allotted for the students to review the material.

NOTES:

_____

_____

_____

_____

_____

_____

_____

_____

_____

_____

_____

_____

_____

_____

_____

Chapter 6

This Is Your Mailbox, That's Your Desk

In this chapter:

Faculty Handbook

Review the faculty handbook or policy manual with your department head before your first class. This is also a good time to ask any additional questions you might have before the class starts (for example, regarding faculty dress codes). The faculty handbook will also help you deal with the "legal stuff."

Legal Stuff

We live in a society in which laws (and lawyers) are a fact of life. The academic world is no exception. As teachers we have to be aware of our legal responsibilities, whether in or out of the classroom. Some of the ways you can make sure you are teaching to the letter as well as the extent of the law is to be mindful of some of the following guidelines.

Cheating: Most schools have a policy concerning cheating by students. Find out what it is, and if you feel it's necessary, include all or part of it in your syllabus.

Following Due Process: **As mentioned above, many universities have academic codes of conduct in which the rules regarding cheating are clearly spelled out. Often, because of the litigious nature of our legal system, professors are not allowed to deal with cases of cheating on their own, but must follow a "due process" procedure laid out by the school. Check with your department head as to how you as a teacher are to handle cases of cheating.**

Sexual harassment: Sexual harassment is a sticky topic and one you do not ever want to become embroiled in. Get a copy of the school's sexual harassment policy and read it carefully.

Your Office Door: **Make sure that when you are talking to students, particularly students of the opposite sex, you keep your office door open at all times. If you need to speak confidentially to a student, do it in the library or in the middle of a noisy cafeteria. If you make an appointment to meet a student before or after class and you don't have an office, meet at the library or in a popular coffee shop. And only meet**

students at your home if there are two or more students you will be meeting with.

Attendance: Check your school's attendance policy. If the school wants you to monitor attendance, it's important that you document all attendance violations with a written record, such as checkmarks on a roster. You never know when it will come in handy.

Attendance by International Students: **In many parts of the world students are not required to attend class. Often, they are only required to pass the tests at the end of the term and hand in the required homework. If attendance is required at your school, make sure your international students understand that they must attend class or face being penalized.**

Students with disabilities: Many schools, and by law all schools that receive federal funding, must comply with Section 504 of the Rehabilitation Act of 1973 and the Americans with Disabilities Act of 1990. You need to be aware of your responsibilities as a teacher in dealing with students who have disabilities. For example, in many cases you are not permitted to refer to a person's disability in the classroom. There may be requirements for your school to provide "note takers" for those students whose disability precludes them taking notes in class. Or a school may be required to provide other reasonable accommodations to meet the needs of disabled students. Many schools have an office of disability services that can help you if you have disabled students in your class requesting additional assistance.

Dating students: This is an easy one. Don't do it! It almost always means trouble for both you and the student. In fact, most schools have policies that clearly define the restrictions on faculty-student relations. This is particularly important where teachers are interacting with nontraditional students who are in their own age group. Ask if your school has such a policy.

Copyright laws: Under the "fair use" exemption of U.S. copyright law, teachers and students are allowed to make copies of text and multimedia materials if they follow certain guidelines and procedures. Ask your supervisor for a copy of the "fair use" exemptions or contact the Library of Congress for a review of the regulations. See the Appendix for the Library of Congress Web site.

***Copying Copyrighted Material:* Under copyright law you can make single copies of printed material for use in your classes without an author's permission. You can also make multiple copies to hand out to your students if you follow certain guidelines. Still, if you are concerned about handing out copies of copyrighted material to your students, put the magazine or book on reserve and let your students make individual copies for their own use.**

Posting grades: The Buckley Amendment makes the posting of grades an invasion of privacy. Today, professors are allowed to give out individual grades only when contacted directly by the student and after having been shown proper identification. It's best not to give grades out over the phone. If a student asks you for a grade over the phone, refer him or her to the office that is responsible for sending out grades at your school. If parents call and asks for their son's or daughter's grade, you have to tell them that by law you are allowed to give that information out only to the student.

***Turning Back Graded Reports:* Don't leave graded reports out in front of your office door for all to see (and compare grades). Hand them back in class or have your students provide you with a stamped, self-addressed envelope that you can use to mail them directly to each student.**

Use the checklists in Chapter 2 to gather the information you might need in order to comply with other school policies and procedures.

Library Privileges

Find out what the library privileges are for part-time teachers. Can you take out books for longer periods of time than students can (many schools offer teachers this option for research purposes)? Find out how to put books on reserve. Because the library plays a crucial role in the academic environment, it's best to find someone at the library you can call on when you need help. Go over and introduce yourself to the head librarian if you have the time.

Grading Policy

You need to find out when final grades are due. With this information you will be better able to plan for the grading of final exams and calculation of final grades. For example, a school may ask that you turn in your grades 48 hours after you give the final exam. Find out the procedure for changing grades in case you need to do so after the final grades have been turned in. You may find that you've made an error, or a student may convince you that he or she did indeed deserve a higher grade. Knowing the procedure in advance will save time.

Teacher Evaluations

In many schools students evaluate teachers during the last week or two of class. Department heads often use these evaluations when deciding whether to rehire part-time teachers. Some schools will have a faculty merit policy that explains how the evaluations by students are used in faculty evaluation. You need to find out how the evaluations are to be administered and how you are to obtain the evaluation forms before class. You also need to find out how and when you can see the results.

 Unbiased Rating: **Don't give a pop quiz and then hand out the evaluation form to your students. If you do, the results will not reflect an unbiased measurement of your teaching abilities.**

Getting Staff Assistance

Is there a secretary who will do clerical work for you? Find out how far in advance you have to submit your material. Find out how you will communicate with your support person if your class meets after the workday ends.

Employment Paperwork

Have you completed your employment paperwork and handed it in to the appropriate department? Have all the required forms been filled out, teaching contracts signed? Do you know how and when you will be paid?

ID Card

Having a faculty ID card can make things easier for you on campus, particularly when using services like the library or school cafeteria. If your supervisor doesn't bring it up first, ask. It just may have slipped his or her mind.

Parking

Find out what your parking privileges are. Find out if you have to pay for parking yourself or if it is part of the teaching package. Find out what parking is available and how difficult it is to get from the closest available parking area to your classroom at the time you are teaching. If at all possible, see if you can park in the "faculty" parking lot, which ensures a parking space when you need it. Faculty lots may also be more strategically located than student lots.

 **Parking Security: If you are teaching a night class, find out what security measures are in place where you are expected to park. This is particularly important if you are alone and have to walk across an empty lot to get to your car. Some schools offer a service where campus security will escort you to your car after a certain hour. This is a nice idea, but can be very time consuming if you have to call and then wait for security to show up at your classroom door.**

Participation in Departmental Activities

Find out if you are expected or invited to attend faculty or departmental meetings. If yes, find out if you are expected to participate in some way or just to observe. It may be difficult for you to participate fully in such meetings because you may not be on campus often enough to know what is happening on a daily basis.

Departmental Meetings and Activities: **Attending campus activities is made more challenging because part-time teachers primarily teach at night and are not available during the day to attend some of the school activities. Do the best you can with the time you have. Ask your department chair or mentor to assist you wherever possible in choosing what activities you should attend.**

NOTES:

_____

_____

_____

_____

_____

_____

_____

_____

_____

_____

Chapter 7

Preparing for Class

In this chapter:

Developing Lesson Plans

The lesson plan is an outline of the material you want to cover in each session. It can be a very quick outline that you follow to help keep the discussion flowing. It can be a detailed set of lecture notes, or it can be a complete outline of each chapter, including lecture notes. Time and experience will dictate what works best for you.

There are a lot of people reading this and thinking, "Oh, no, not lesson plans. I don't have time to sit down and make out a detailed lesson plan for each class!" *Do you have the time to jot down a half-page lesson plan?* It can be as simple as that.

In the heat of battle teachers can forget key points they want to make, particularly if they don't have something in front of them to act as a reminder. To avoid this problem, briefly list the subjects you want to cover in the upcoming class. You should include the "housekeeping" items you need to deal with, like taking attendance, giving a quiz, or discussing next week's assignment. You can include comments you want to make that are not in your lecture notes that might concern a more current application of the subject matter to be discussed. If you want to be sure to respond to a particular student's question asked during a previous class, you can note the student's name on the lesson plan as a reminder. Once you know all you want to cover, make a simple task list and put it in the order in which you want to cover the items.

A simple lesson plan might include the following:

1. General housekeeping (attendance, handing back old tests, etc.)
2. Handing out new materials for future action
3. Giving an assignment for the next class
4. Review of the major concepts discussed in the last class
5. Quick overview of concepts to be discussed in this class
6. Class presentation/lecture/discussion and other learning activities
7. Quick review of subject matter just discussed.

It's always best to give assignments at the beginning of class rather than at the end. Students are more focused at the beginning of class and are more likely to write down the assignment for future reference. Write out all major assignments and hand them out to the class. This helps ensure there is no miscommunication between you and the students. The more detailed the assignment sheet, the better job the students will do in following it.

Your lesson plan can be as simple as the following:

Finance 2004
September 25, 2000

1. Take attendance.
2. Ask for last week's homework.
3. Give handouts on new financing instrument available at U.S. banks, ask that students review for class in two weeks.
4. Next week's assignment, chapter 5 and Hegronomy Inc. case and questions.
5. Reminder: exam in two weeks.
6. Review of today's class:
   - New corporate business cycle financing
   - How a company can reduce risks in today's business climate
   - Actual successes in hedging risk.
7. Discuss chapter 4, A New Financial Age, pages 247-265.
8. Students are to break up into 3 groups and for 10 minutes discuss the Argon Ltd. case. Each group is to give a 5-minute presentation on the core problem facing Argon as well as possible solutions to the problem.
9. (If time allows) Review the major points discussed during class.

Computer Help: **If you put your class plan on your word processor, it's simple to update the plan for your next class. Just pull up the last plan, update it to reflect the next class, and save it to the file with just a quick two digit date change in the file name. For example, ClassPlan101700.doc (October 17, 2000) is saved as ClassPlan101900.doc by changing the 17 to a 19 and resaving it.**

Review, Review, Review: **Notice in the example above that the teacher reviews material that was presented in a previous class or talks about the material about to be presented. This may seem like overkill, but it's important. Reviewing material reinforces the learning process. It also helps students visualize how the material fits into the big picture. For material currently under discussion, reviewing helps put it into the context of what has already been discussed. We will talk more about this in the section on motivation and learning.**

What's a Chapter Outline?

If your lectures and presentations follow the structure of the textbook, developing chapter outlines on which your students can make notes can be helpful to the learning process. And if you can write your lecture notes around the outlines, it helps to ensure that both you and the students are on the same wavelength. This is particularly true for introductory classes or classes where students do not have strong learning skills coming into the course.

Why use chapter outlines?

From the student's point of view, using chapter outlines can minimize the time students spend in class writing down basic information from your lecture, allowing them more time to participate in the classroom discussion. From the teacher's point of view, chapter outlines help you know where you are going and allow you to plan each lesson around a fixed amount of material. If handed out (or sent by email) ahead of class time, students can write notes on the outline as they study the material prior to class to ensure that they are ready to join in the class discussion of the material. You can also use outlines to alert students to what is particularly critical in their readings for the next class discussion or exam. Whether you use chapter outlines depends on the size of the class and the time you have to put into developing them.

What's in it for you?

Structure: Outlines force you to look at how the information is structured in the book. You may find that you have to structure your presentations and discussions differently to meet a particular book's format. Remember that students depend on the book and other assigned readings to give them the information they either did not understand in class, or that was not covered in class. This said, many students don't use the textbook enough as a learning tool. Often they don't take the time to read the material, or they depend on the classroom presentation for the information they need. Sometimes the teacher does not include enough of the textbook material in his or her own presentations to make it worthwhile (in the student's eyes) to buy the book. By following an outline, you will help students better organize all the information they read, write, and evaluate during the term, no matter the source. And, when using an outline, both teachers and students know where they are in the learning process.

Flow: Using outlines helps you develop a flow of information that is a mixture of the information found in the text and your real-world experiences. If you feel the information provided in the book is not adequate to cover the subject, using an outline allows you to insert pertinent information into your presentation in a logical manner. When first starting out, your notes may tend to be overly wordy. Don't worry. Your need for detailed notes will probably diminish as you get more comfortable with teaching and with the subject matter.

Thinking ahead: Using outlines lets you think ahead about the information to be covered and the amount of discussion and interchange you can allow and still meet the time constraints of the class.

Time management: Should the lack of class time remaining in the term become a factor, outlines allow you to identify those areas ahead of time that you can tell the students to cover outside of class, to review only briefly, or to skip altogether.

An example of a simple outline using chapter headings in a textbook follows. Where you want to ensure that students understand a particular word or concept that is not a chapter heading, you can add it in using a "[DEF]," or definition statement.

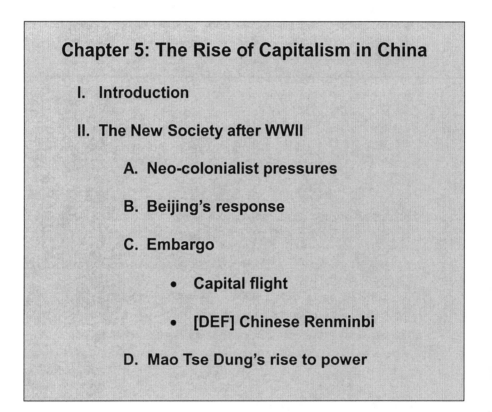

Chapter 5: The Rise of Capitalism in China

I. Introduction

II. The New Society after WWII

    A. Neo-colonialist pressures

    B. Beijing's response

    C. Embargo

- Capital flight

- [DEF] Chinese Renminbi

    D. Mao Tse Dung's rise to power

Type Size: Outlines can simply be the chapter headings, subheadings, and topic prompts as they are laid out in the textbook. To provide a sufficient amount of blank white space in which students can write notes, the font type should be at least 18 point.

Creating Lecture Notes: You can easily create your own lecture notes by adding a number of spaces between each line of the chapter outline and writing your lecture notes in that space.

Publisher's Outlines: Some textbook publishers offer chapter outlines in the instructor's manual/resource guide. As with other publisher supplied material, make sure you evaluate the quality of these outlines before you use them.

This Info Not in Book: You can add information to an outline that is not in the book, but you should note this on the outline so the student will not waste time looking through the book for it. You can add the phrase "(not in text)" to indicate when you have added new information to a textbook outline.

Problems using outlines

When using outlines you will be faced with a dilemma that has plagued teachers from time immemorial. Students will say to you, "My time is better spent if you (the teacher) lecture first on the material in a chapter and then I go back and reread the chapter to make sure I understand the details." If you decide to structure your class this way, most students will wait until you have lectured on a chapter before they read it. If, as most teachers agree, repetition is one of the bedrocks of learning, you need to motivate students to read the chapter before coming to class, not after you have presented the material in class. If you use outlines and you do not motivate students to study the chapter before class, students will use the outlines as a crutch, and your classes will quickly turn into straight lectures with little discussion possible (since the students have not read the chapter before class).

One way to motivate your students to read material before class is to assign homework that is due before the material is discussed in class. Ask your students to answer a certain number of questions at the end of each chapter or write up a short paper or case that reflects the application of the material in the chapter – before class.

Another option: question outlines

Another way to structure your course is to develop an outline that is a series of questions. These are questions that cover the material you feel the students should focus on as they study the text or other materials. You can tell your students that if they read the chapter and answer the questions you have asked in your "outline," they will have a pretty good idea of what you consider to be most important in the chapter (and what will probably be on the test).

You can pass out the questions as study guides prior to the class that will be discussing the topic and tell your students that they are to come to class having answered the questions and prepared to discuss them in class. Some teachers also tell the class that because it is difficult to generate a good two-way discussion if students have not read the material beforehand, if a student cannot answer a question from the list of questions satisfactorily, the student loses one point of his or her participation grade. Answering a question "satisfactorily" in this case means:

A. Student answers the question correctly.

B. Student is not entirely correct, but his or her answer indicates he or she read the material, but just didn't understand it.

C. Student reads the answer, or part of the answer from written notes prepared before class.

Reading the answer from the book is not a satisfactory answer!

Referring back to the outline earlier in this chapter, the questions given to students might be those in the example on the next page.

Chapter 5: The Rise of Capitalism in China

1. How does the rise of capitalism in China affect the global economy today?

2. During the neo-colonialist period there were many pressures facing the Chinese people. Describe three of those pressures and how they helped formed the society after WWII.

3. The Beijing government responded to the neo-colonialist pressures in three ways. What were they?

4. What was the effect of the U.S. government embargo on Chinese exports? How did it effect the value of the Chinese currency?

5. What were the factors following the rejection of neo-colonialism that led to the rise of Mao Tse Dung?

You can use these questions as an outline when developing your classroom presentation, just as you would with the earlier outline.

When to Assign Outside Work: **If you assign homework (chapter assignments, short papers, cases, etc.) after discussing the subject in class, everyone should, theoretically, get a perfect score, and you will have lost a learning opportunity. Students need to study the material before the class in which it is discussed to minimize class time devoted to lecturing and maximize the use of more productive learning activities. Therefore, assign homework that is to be completed <u>before</u> the corresponding class discussion. A word of caution, though. You must be ready to accept responses that are less than perfect. For many the material will be brand new and require some class discussion before its meaning becomes completely clear.**

Student Surveys

Some teachers find it useful to develop student surveys the students fill out during the first class. These surveys provide the teacher with basic background information like the student's major and class standing (junior, senior, etc.) as well as background information that may be pertinent to the class. You can then ask the student to contribute his or her particular knowledge to the class discussions. Another reason for using a student survey is to ask students for phone numbers and email addresses through which they can be reached. Since part-time teachers are not on campus as often as full-time teachers, it is important for them to have a way of contacting their students outside of the classroom should the need arise. Some of the questions you might want to ask in the student survey are:

- Name
- Home phone number
- Email address (the one they use most often)
- Class standing
- Major
- Previous classes taken in the subject area
- Language capabilities (for international students)
- Country of birth (for international students)
- Hours they spend per week in outside jobs
- Total class load that term (e.g. 18 hours)
- Any questions they would like to have answered as a result of taking the course.

Run the survey past your department head before giving it to your students to ensure there are no legal barriers to asking this information of your students.

What To Take With You

Once the administrative paperwork is completed, you have your textbook, and you know that the audiovisual equipment will be available when you need it, it's time to get ready for your first class.

Some of the things you should take with you into your first class are listed below; others may be required depending on your particular subject area:

A. Detailed syllabus

B. Current student roster (if available for first class)

C. Textbook

D. Class plan

E. Student survey (optional)

F. Emergency teaching supplies (chalk, markers, etc.)

G. Outline or lecture notes

H. Assignment(s) for the next class

I. Instructional aids (overheads, video, handouts, etc.)

J. Opening remarks (for first class)

K. *A SMILE!*

Your First Class

First impressions: Most part-time teachers have a strong practical grasp of their subject matter, but when they get in front of a class for the first time and try to translate that information into a presentation or discussion, they may not do well the first time out. First impressions do count. The better prepared and organized you are for the first class, the more the students will respect you as the class progresses. Many teachers use the first class to set the tone for the term. Teachers also use the first class to establish a "team" atmosphere in which both the students and the teacher understand that they have equal responsibility in establishing a positive learning environment.

Rehearsing: Before you meet with your first class, it's always best to rehearse (several times) the presentation of the material you plan to discuss. Even if you have taught in the past, you should review your notes to determine how much time your presentation may take this time around. This is particularly true if you have changed texts or added new material since your last teaching assignment. If you are concerned about not having enough material to cover in the time allotted, bring more than you think is necessary. It's always best to err on the side of having two much information rather than too little. Remember that the questions at the end of the chapters are often excellent sources of discussion material. And always try to have the next class' material ready (and with you), in case you find there is time to begin discussion of this new topic before the class period ends.

You're the boss: It's a crude way of putting it, but it's true. New part-time people often get into trouble in the classroom when they let the control of the class pass to the students. The school expects part-time teachers, as well as their full-time counterparts, to manage their classrooms in an effective way. Students have rights, but so do teachers. Teachers have the right to determine what is done, and not done, in the classroom. Don't let that right pass to others.

Don't kiss off your first class: The first class sets the tone for all the classes that follow. Make sure you use all the time allotted. If you let the students out early during your first class, it will give them the impression that they can expect the same in the future. Because some students may drop your course after the first class, and others may add it, you might want to discuss subjects that are more general than you might discuss in subsequent classes. You will surely be discussing the points on the syllabus during your first class. You can also use the first class to show how the subject matter relates to the big picture of the world in general. You can use the first class to go over the introductory chapter in the text. Or, you can do something to engage the students that will set a tone for the classes to follow. You might want to announce to your students during the first class that you will be keeping them the whole time. This will ensure that your students know the importance you place on the time spent in class. The students should leave the first class feeling they have already learned something of importance regarding your subject.

Each class different: In some classes you will have students who are very interested in discussing a particular subject, and in others you will find that there is much less interest. It's helpful to review the roster before class for any information on the type of students who will be attending your class. What are their class standings (sophomore, junior, etc.), their majors, are they traditional or nontraditional students, etc.? Any additional information, like past classes taken, that you can obtain from the registrar's office will also help you get some idea as to the type of students you will have in your class.

Extra Syllabi: **Be prepared to see new faces in your first few classes as students drop and add your course. Make sure you have extra syllabi handy for these new students so they can quickly catch up to their colleagues.**

Your Own "Teaching Resource Guide"

Most teachers are not born good teachers. They develop their skills over many years of practice. This manual will help you get a jump-start on the learning process by showing you what has worked well for teachers in the past (and what has not). You can then determine, through your own classroom experience, what works best for you.

One of the ways you can help the process along is by starting your own "Teaching Resource Guide." This is a file or notebook in which you keep all materials related to your teaching experience. As you begin developing your own teaching style, the material you amass in the notebook will help you decide what works best for you. This should include copies of articles you have referred to in class, old class plans, particularly good questions your students asked, relevant overheads (and notes on what points you made using them), old tests and quizzes, etc.

What If You Have To Miss a Class?

If you know there is a possibility you will not be able to make an upcoming class, and you know you cannot get a substitute teacher on short notice, do the following. Generate an "In-Class Exercise" sheet that asks questions about the topics that you would have been going over in the chapter that day, had you been there. Then give the In-Class Exercise to someone in your department (chairperson, mentor, another teacher) who can hand it out to the class should you not be able to teach that day. Have your students answer the questions and turn them in before they leave the building. It's best if you can ask one of your colleagues to remain in the classroom while your students answer the questions. By using In-Class Exercises, students do not waste their time coming to your class even though you have been called away. In addition, you are able to pass on to the students an idea of what you feel is most important in a particular chapter, and the students have the opportunity of getting in some quality study time.

Make sure your directions on the In-Class Exercise are crystal clear and detailed. You don't want students to have to ask questions of the person handing out the exercise. And make sure you give the following information in advance to your colleague so that he or she can inform your students at the beginning of class:

- When you will be returning to class.
- When students should turn in any materials originally assigned for this class.
- What the class will be discussing (or what material the class will be responsible for knowing) when you return.
- What to do if students have any additional questions (for example, they should hold any questions until your return).
- How much extra credit the In-Class Exercise is worth (although not required, probably advisable – see following).
- Whether students can use their own books or notes to complete the exercise.

- Whether students can work with other students in class to complete the exercise. NOTE: If you want them to work alone, but some students ignore the rules and begin to talk among themselves, it could put the person administering the exercise in a difficult position. It's unrealistic to ask neutral administrators to enforce rules you set down but are not there to enforce. Tell the administrator that if students decide to ignore the announced rules the administrators should ignore the infractions.
- What students are to do if they did not bring books or notes to class that your exercise requires they use. For example, if a student didn't bring a textbook, he or she should ask another student to share. Or if this is not possible, the students should note on the In-Class Exercise that no text was available, and answer the questions to the best of his or her ability.
- What the consequences (if any) are should a student not want to stay and complete the exercise. This is up to you. If the question comes up, you shouldn't insist that everyone has to stay and do the exercise because that puts the person administering the test in the role of class policeman. If you assign extra points, then the consequences are simple: The student does not get the extra points. NOTE: You should tell the administrator what the consequences are and let him or her decide when to use this information. This is only to assist the administrator should the question arise. If no one asks to leave, it's a moot point.
- To whom students are to turn in the completed exercise and when.

Now it's time for class!

NOTES:

Part III

In the Classroom

Chapter 8

How Students Learn

In this chapter:

Learning Theory

Learning theory has been the subject of many books and articles. Names like Robert Gagne and Robert Mager figure heavily in this literature. We will not cover learning theory as such in this manual, although many of the topics discussed are related in some way, shape, or form to applied learning theory and its structural components. If you are interested in learning more about these theories and their application in the classroom, please refer to books by these authors and their contemporaries listed in the Appendix.

Learning Styles

There are almost as many student learning styles as there are students. Neil Fleming, while at Lincoln University in New Zealand, developed a popular inventory that students and teachers alike can use to identify four basic learning preferences. The VARK (Visual, Aural, Read/write, Kinesthetic) inventory helps explain how people take in information. If you understand these four basic styles before you begin interacting with students, it will enable you to adapt your teaching style to a much larger number of students.

Visual Style

The visual student prefers to "see" the material he or she is expected to learn. They prefer to use charts, graphs, symbols, pictures, illustrated textbooks, videos, and similar learning aids to understand the material rather than just having it presented via the written word or as an oral presentation. They want to be able to see the big picture, to understand the material with all its facets and nuances.

Aural (listening) style

Students who need to hear the material use the listening style of learning. These students depend on clear, well thought out presentations and discussions to learn the material required to meet the course objectives. They want to discuss the material with other students and professors, and they depend on memory recall to tie the material together. They tend to summarize their notes rather than write everything you say down in great detail. Listening is more important to their learning process than writing or reading.

Read/write style

Students who need to read or write something to learn it respond to the traditional picture of the teacher-student relationship. These students learn through taking detailed notes in class and by using printed material (textbooks, dictionaries, handouts, lecture notes, etc.) when studying outside the classroom setting. They rely on memorizing lists of information, notes, and the rewriting of critical facts to help them learn the subject matter.

Kinesthetic style

The kinesthetic student relies on "doing" to facilitate the learning process. Students who prefer the kinesthetic style use all their senses to understand the information before them. They like lab exercises and field trips in which they can see, touch, taste, feel, and hear the subjects under discussion. They like teachers who can apply the material to examples in everyday life. These students have a hard time just listening to a lecture. They need to be involved in the process.

And the winner is?

Sorry to disappoint you, but there is no clear winner. Since the different styles are generally distributed equally throughout the student population (in fact, some students use multiple styles simultaneously), the more styles you can address, the more learning will take place. Many experts recommend that teachers vary their teaching style every 20 minutes in order to meet the needs of as many students as possible and to make the learning process more enjoyable for all students.

It's important to remember that one's teaching style tends to be related to one's own learning style. Although it's difficult to generalize across all professions, many teachers in higher education tend to favor the read/write style of learning. They often want students to use lectures and library research to help them understand the material. Unfortunately, this leaves out those students who might favor one of the other three styles, or who may be multi-modal (have multiple preferences). Teachers need to determine what kind of learning style they favor before they begin teaching and adjust their teaching style to include the three other styles.

 VARK On-line: **Teachers and students alike can learn what learning style they respond to best by taking the VARK inventory. It's free of charge and can be found at the following Web site: www.active-learning-site.com/vark.htm.**

Traditional Students

These are the students who often enter college just out of high school and who intend to go straight through school carrying a full course load. Some are highly motivated while some are not. It depends on the class, the academic level of the student (freshmen, junior, master's, etc.) and the student's reasons for attending school. Because traditional students are usually in their late teens and early 20s, they are quick to pick up concepts and can memorize key facts relatively easily. The challenge is that they usually have had no practical experience against which to compare and analyze what they are learning.

Nontraditional Students

These are students whose abilities and ages vary widely. They are often coming back to school after being in the workplace for a number of years and studying part-time to earn a degree. Because they are, on average, older than traditional students, they will not be as good at memorizing and recalling information as their younger counterparts. Age reduces the capacity of the brain to retain information. Yet, they are often more serious about the learning process and more focussed on the completion of course material and the application of that material to the workplace. They can also analyze information more effectively and see patterns and systems better than their younger counterparts. The challenge is that many distractions (family, job, financial problems, etc.) outside of class can have a significant effect on their performance in class. You will need to be a good motivator to hold their attention.

You may also encounter nontraditional students who know more about a particular subject than you do because of the experience they may have had in the workplace. In this case you need to be able to accept their expertise and use it to the benefit of the class without letting them dominate the discussion.

The Continuing Education Student

As our population ages, students are going back to school for a number of reasons, not just to finish an interrupted course of study towards a degree. Many continuing ed students are going back to school simply to upgrade their current skills or to learn new ones. Others are going back to school after retirement to keep their minds active and themselves engaged. An increasing number of schools are setting up separate continuing education programs, sometimes called "shadow colleges" to meet the needs of these students. Schools are having to reinvent how information is taught to continuing ed students.

The regular Monday through Friday class structure is also being challenged by the demands of continuing ed students. Grades (and degrees) do not motivate many of these "life-long learners" as much as they do traditional students. They are there to learn something new or different. And they expect you to provide them with this information. These students can be very demanding about the quality of the information presented and how well the teacher relates the information to the world outside the classroom. Even though they may not consider a good grade a top priority, never underestimate the drive or dedication of continuing education students. Be prepared for a stimulating and interesting classroom.

Students with an Attitude

You will come into contact with all kinds of students, many of whom are serious about school and willing to put the time into study and coursework necessary to meet the requirements of the course. But there are always one or two students in every class who can make your classroom experience challenging.

The student who can't stop arguing: Sometimes you will have a student who does not agree with you on a particular subject and insists on pointing it out in class over and over again. Whether this is a traditional or nontraditional student, the best place to handle this kind of discussion is outside of the classroom. Then you and the student can sit down one-on-one and find out what the problem is and look for solutions.

The "know-it-all": You may have a student in your class who thinks he or she knows it all and blurts out an answer every time you ask a question. You must make sure that the know-it-all does not negatively influence the rest of the students by continually jumping in with answers. One way to minimize this is to let students know early on that you are in control of the class. This may mean you have to call on specific students and then ask your questions, rather than asking the class in a general way.

To move the center of attention away from a know-it-all and give others a chance to respond, you might want to use a phrase like, "John, let's see what some other folks think." If that doesn't give the know-it-all the hint, you may have to suggest after class (and in a supportive way) that he or she let others answer questions in the future to give everyone a chance to participate.

The boss: You may also encounter the student who has not been in the classroom for a number of years and is not comfortable in a student's role. He or she may be the boss at work and have a hard time making the transition to the more subservient role of student. Be patient, but do not compromise your role as teacher by agreeing to let this type of student take over your class. At some time this person will have to learn what it means to be a student in an academic environment. It might as well be you who begins the process.

The disinterested: Trying to motivate a student who will not participate in class discussions can be very discouraging. This student could be naturally shy or may simply not be interested in the material. Foreign-born students have a particularly difficult time opening up in front of a class full of American students. As a teacher you want to motivate as many of your students as you can. A lot will depend on your own particular teaching style. But, even the best teacher in the world can't motivate everyone. So, don't feel bad if "Mr. Disinterested" can't be motivated to become part of the class discussion (and risk a poor participation grade). It comes with the territory.

The great excuse maker: Students are going to come to you with excuses that are right out of fantasyland. They will complain about things that make absolutely no sense to you. It's up to you to figure out the best way to deal with each new excuse, no matter how far-fetched it seems. Your supervisor doesn't have the time to make the decisions for you. Do the best you can and move on.

Stay After Class a Few Minutes: **Remain in the classroom for several minutes after class to let the students know you are willing to stick around for questions if the students need additional help or direction, or if they are too embarrassed to ask a question during the regular class period.**

International Students

The number of international students entering U.S. institutions of higher learning has increased dramatically over the last ten years. These students pose a particular problem for teachers in that not only are these students' skills all over the board, but their level of comprehension of the English language is quite varied as well. There is also a large group of naturalized Americans (of Vietnamese, Chinese, and Mexican roots, to name a few) who have similar challenges in the classroom. In this manual we will use the term "international student" to refer to both foreign students who intend to complete their schooling and return to their native country and students born in another country who are permanent residents of the United States.

Cultural issues: The problems facing international students in U.S. schools are often the result of a mixture of language and cultural differences. As a general rule, American students are individualists who are often able to make decisions alone, without consulting others. They are not afraid to question professors if they feel there is a problem. On the other hand, many international students come from cultures where professors are put on a pedestal and where no one questions a professor's presentation or intent. In other cultures, decisions are made as a group rather than individually. Individual thought is not something students from these cultures are comfortable with. In either case you will need to find a way to get past these cultural barriers and help those from other cultures learn how they need to respond in this culture. After all, when in Rome…. Only then will they be successful in the U.S. learning environment.

Minimize Cultural Bias: **When preparing for your class, review the examples you plan to give in class and try to minimize those that are culturally biased. For instance, you may use an example in class where you relate the story of a person going into a store and buying a bottle of Clorox®. To American students this is not a problem, but to foreign students from countries where Clorox® is not a household name, the term may not be understood. In this case using the generic word "bleach" would serve you better. Slang is also culturally based, so try to minimize its use whenever possible.**

Relate Subject To Student's Culture: **To get international students more involved in the classroom discussion, ask them a question about some subject you are studying and how it relates to their culture. This will give them something to respond to that they are comfortable with.**

Turn to the CIA: **If you want to know more about a particular country and its people, a good starting point is the CIA country database. See the Appendix for the Web site.**

The "language" question: Besides understanding the classroom environment, students have to understand the material as well. For many foreign students this involves mastering the idiomatic English that it is presented in. If you have a large number of international students in your class, put as much as you can on the board or on overheads so foreign students can copy down the words, even if they don't understand them, and look them up after class. International students benefit from both hearing and seeing the word or concept under discussion. They also appreciate outlines that can help them organize and categorize the new material in their own minds. An international student will often refer back to the textbook to ensure he or she understood the material presented in class. A good textbook and a presentation style that follows the book's structure are critical to a quality learning experience for these students.

Start Out Speaking Slowly: **One way to help your international students keep up with the class presentation is to make sure you speak slowly for the first few classes. This will give them a chance to become accustomed to your speaking style. Many will have learned British English rather than U.S. English in school, and it will take them a few classes to get used to your American accent.**

Assessing English Levels: **Assess the English proficiency of your international students early on in the term. One way to do this is to set up a get-acquainted session with each foreign student and listen to him or her talk about the past and goals for the future. Then you can decide how much outside help that student might need or whether he or she has the skills necessary to succeed in your class.**

What's the problem? International students can be a challenge for teachers because it is sometimes very difficult to understand the source of a problem in class. It could be related to language, to culture, or both. In addition, international students may have very different expectations than those of their U.S. counterparts as to what they want to accomplish during their college or university experience in the United States. The more you can learn about their backgrounds, the better you will be able to understand any problems that arise.

Loss-of-face issues: Many international students would never admit to you that they do not understand something you are discussing in class. This would mean "losing face" in their own culture. You might want to ask a student to paraphrase something you suspect they do not understand – but do it gently and with a smile. Don't say, "No, that's not right." Rather, try to reduce response stress by asking, "Can anyone think of another way of putting it?" or by responding, "Not quite, but close."

You can also contact foreign students after class and ask them to meet with you to discuss some of the problems in comprehension they may be having. In fact, you may find that international students are much more comfortable discussing a problem with you one-on-one than in discussing the problem with you in class. But, in many cases you will have to make the first move.

Smile ☺*:* **Americans can be very intimidating to people from other cultures. When working with international students, always smile. It's the international sign that lets students know that you are there to help, not hassle.**

Get the Name Right: **A person's name is a very personal thing. Americanizing a person's name, such as substituting John for Jacque, can be insulting to an international student. Imagine how you would feel if someone changed your name without your permission. Try to learn the foreign students' names as pronounced in their languages. This shows that you have respect for the students and where they come from. Only if a student offers you the option of using an Americanized name should you use one.**

Gender Issues

Teachers today have to be sensitive to gender bias and how it can affect a student's self-image in the classroom. Teachers can be unconsciously stereotyping students without realizing it. They need to present material that is as all-inclusive as possible. For example, a teacher may unconsciously be using the pronoun "he" in all of the examples used in class. Try to use both "he" and "she" interchangeably. Get feedback from your students if you feel this may be the case in your classroom. Or record one of your classes and listen to how you use the gender pronouns. Also, if you use cases in class, try to use cases that portray both men and women in similar positions.

Are You Getting Through?

There are any number of ways you can motivate students to learn. In the section on evaluation we will tie learning styles to methods of evaluating students. If you do a good job in evaluating your students you will also know how successful you have been in motivating your students to learn. Competent evaluation can also help point out any areas where you might need to brush up on your own teaching skills.

You Are Teacher, They Are Students: **It is important to remember that you have a job to do. Do not sacrifice the scope of your course's content or integrity in an effort to get the students to like you. You are the teacher – they are the students! You are there to teach, not to be well liked. Watch out what you agree to change during the term to meet students' needs or demands. Think first about how it meets your needs as a teacher.**

Basic Learning Tools

Using Projects

Many teachers, in an effort to give students a taste of the world outside of the classroom, will ask their students to complete some kind of project. This is often done as a group. Many teachers also ask their students to present the final project in class. If structured correctly a project can indeed be an excellent application of classroom learning to real-world applications. On the other hand, if structure and planning are not built into the project assignment from the beginning, projects can be a waste of time for both student and teacher.

Projects can work well or not at all, depending on the makeup of the project team, the subject to be researched, and how the project activities are structured. It's critical that if you are asking your students to break up into teams, that the project assigned is complex enough to demand a team effort. Always keep in mind that grading projects can be very time-consuming for the teacher. Make sure you have allowed yourself enough time to grade them.

Assigning projects: Some things to consider when assigning projects are:

✓ Group projects introduce students to the concept of work groups and the dynamics of working within a team setting. For projects to be considered successful, students need to demonstrate that they have learned something they would not have learned in the classroom. There are several challenges in assigning group projects (also referred to as team projects) that need to be addressed.

1. Students are students. The majority tends to wait until the last minute to complete a project. A system of "milestones" needs to be set by the teacher to ensure that students are working on the project throughout the term. These milestones should be included in the syllabus (see syllabus example in Chapter 4).

2. Teachers often overestimate the capability of students when assigning projects, particularly when the students are traditional, undergraduate students. Most students do not have the analytical or professional writing skills to generate professional quality work, particularly the kind of work part-time teachers are used to seeing outside of the classroom. This is something the teacher is going to have to take into account when grading project work. This is also an area where the teacher can make a real impact on a student's life, by helping the student realize where his or her weaknesses are and finding help (outside tutoring, school supported training programs, etc.) to begin correcting the problem.

3. In team projects, there are often those in the team who do the lion's share of the work and others who hang back and let them do it. To fairly evaluate project work, many teachers have each team member rate his or her efforts as well as that of his or her colleagues. The teacher then takes this into consideration at grading time. See Chapter 14, for a more in-depth explanation of how to evaluate students working on group projects.

✓ Teachers should never assume that students know how to work in groups. Teachers need to take time in class to talk about the responsibilities that members of a group have. If the group project is a major portion of a student's grade, one class period should be set aside for explaining the teamwork and responsibilities involved in group projects and the expected results. Always find out from your students how many of them have worked on group projects before.

✓ Try to limit groups to a maximum of three to four students per group. Larger groups become unwieldy and hinder both student performance and the teacher's ability to fairly evaluate both the individual and group performance.

Discussion points: Students often benefit from a review of what the keys to good group work are before a group project is assigned. This discussion can include:

✓ A review of how the group will work together over the project period to accomplish the project goals. For example, a project could be broken up into four segments, the team members will meet every two weeks, and a draft of the project will be completed three weeks before the final exam.

✓ What the group will do if one of the group members is not carrying his or her workload and at what point the group is going to let the team member know that his or her work is not satisfactory.

✓ The need to record attendance at all group meetings.

✓ The self-assessment skills each group will need to consider when assigning tasks to individual team members (e.g. the best writer, best researcher, best facilitator, best presenter, etc.).

✓ The critical information to exchange, such as phone numbers, email addresses, and available meeting times.

T I P

Group Think: Once students are assigned to a particular group, you might ask that they change their seats to be closer to other group members. This will help them start thinking and working as a group. At the first in-class group meeting, have each group make up a sheet with member's names, addresses, and phone numbers. The group should assign one group member the task of photocopying the information sheet and sending it to the other members of the group. Please note that this seating arrangement may require that you be extra vigilant during test taking time. This is to minimize any cheating that might occur because of the close relationships that have been formed as a result of the project teamwork.

T I P

Meeting Group Timetables: The project team needs to provide you with written or oral proof that they are meeting your timetable for completion. You might want to tie these timelines to the material being covered in class. Also, try to plan it so the project is due one or two weeks before final exams so students won't be trying to study for exams and completing your project (and those of other teachers) all at the same time.

Group Projects and Nontraditional Students: For nontraditional students, group projects are a bigger challenge than for traditional students. Since most of these students work during the day, it is often difficult for them to meet outside of the classroom. If it's necessary to assign a project in a class of nontraditional students, leave it up to the teams as to when and where they should meet. Or, if time allows, give students the last 20 minutes of each class period to work on team projects.

Using Guest Speakers

Guest speakers can be a good way to bring the world of work into the classroom. Yet, there are some things you need to consider when using guest speakers to make the experience a positive one for both the speaker and the students.

Prepare speakers in advance: Some guest speakers will not be comfortable being confined by the limited class time schedules students and teachers have to adhere to. In addition, students often want to ask lots of questions of speakers. Just the introduction and the concluding remarks can take up an inordinate amount of time. In addition, speakers enjoy telling war stories, which can eat up a lot of valuable class time. Therefore, you need to prepare the speaker in advance as to what you are covering in class and what points you would like him or her to reinforce during the presentation. You also want to give your guest speaker very specific time limits.

Get references: Being a seasoned professional does not mean a speaker has the skills to motivate students to learn. Try to get references from people who have heard a prospective presenter speak in the past.

Prepare for no-shows: Speakers sometimes don't show up due to last minute work commitments, emergencies, etc. You should always have additional material ready to discuss should this happen in your class.

Find the speaker's niche: Speakers are usually more appropriate for advanced classes where the subject of the presentation can be more focussed. The use of outside speakers will depend to some extent on your own experience outside of the classroom. Your experience may be as interesting as an outside speaker's, or even more so since you can probably tie it back to the subject matter more effectively.

Second Best: **Speakers who have to cancel out will sometimes ask if they can send someone else as a replacement. Unfortunately, this may not always be the best solution because you do not have time to review the background information on the replacement. The replacement may be a much poorer speaker than the originally scheduled speaker. If it's not too awkward, you may want to ask if you can reschedule rather than accept a stand-in. Tell them they come so highly recommended that anything less than the best is just not acceptable.**

Using Cases

A case is a description of a real-life situation or a fictitious representation of what could be a real-life situation. By analyzing cases, students are given the opportunity of understanding and solving problems they may confront in the world outside the classroom. Unfortunately, many students do not know how to analyze cases effectively. We'll offer some tips below that can help you use cases more effectively in your classroom.

Cases can be used in a number of ways. Two of the most common are:

1. **As classroom discussion:** A case can be used in a classroom discussion assignment where students are required to respond to the problems and situations illustrated in the case. Each student is then evaluated on his or her understanding of the case and analysis of the contents.

2. **As homework:** A case can be used as a homework assignment where the students are to analyze a case and turn in a review of that analysis. Once the graded assignment is returned to the students, the whole class can discuss the results.

You need to talk with your students early on to determine how much casework they have done in the past. Your chairperson or mentor can also give you an idea of how often the case method is used as a teaching tool in your school.

The task before you is to prevent your course from being one on teaching students "how to do cases." Rather, you want to focus on the case material as a bridge from the textbook to the real world. You may want to give your students the following review of the case method to help them understand casework better.

A review of the case method

Objectives for using cases:

 Learning by doing.

 Participation in a real-life situation.

 Application of theory to actual problems.

✔ Development of analytical and problem-solving skills.

Tactics used by students to analyze cases:

✔ Isolate the "real" problem(s) from problems that really have little or no bearing on the case.

✔ Propose viable solution(s) to the "real" problem(s) only.

✔ Evaluate the outcomes and consequences of a decision(s) that has already been made in the case, or one that the student proposes and must then defend.

Methodology students should use to analyze cases:

1. Determine from whose point of view students are looking at the problem or problems.

2. Identify the "real" problem(s).

3. Identify the "real" causes of the real problem(s).

4. If they are not already presented, determine alternative solutions to the real problem(s).

5. Select the best solution to the real problem(s).

6. Develop an action plan to implement the best solution.

Tips:

✔ Students should give a case a general reading and then put it aside for a few hours. They should then read it a second time and make notes on critical facts. Once they understand the critical facts of the case, they should then prepare the written analysis.

✔ Students should be cautioned not to jump to conclusions.

✔ Students should not expect a case to contain all the information that they would expect to have in the real world. If they feel that additional information can be found to make the case analysis more meaningful and relevant, and the information is readily available, then they should be encouraged to add the information. If not, then they should assume that the information given in the case is sufficient to develop a reasonable solution. The teacher needs to state the information availability parameters up front.

✓ Although some solutions are better than others, students should realize there are often no right or wrong answers in cases because situations in the real world can change from moment to moment.

Adapted from "A Model for Analyzing Cases" by Dr. Stella Nkomo

Case worksheets

Many students look at a case as a situation where someone else is making a decision and the student has to decide what someone else's decision might be. This is not the optimum way to begin analyzing a case. Rather, it's important that from the very beginning students understand that they are to make decisions as if they were in the place of the central "character" in the case (company president, leader of the country, circuit court judge, etc.). To accomplish this the students need to answer the question, "Who Am I?" before beginning to work on the case. Answering this question correctly helps students put themselves in place of the main problem solver. Once this is accomplished they can begin looking at real-world problems and solutions. A case worksheet can help organize a student's thoughts while working through a case. A sample case worksheet follows.

CASE WORKSHEET

STUDENT: _____

DATE: _____/_____/_____

CASE: _____

WHO AM I? _____

Identify the major problem(s) (circle the #1 problem):

1. _____
2. _____
3. _____

Identify the causes of the #1 problem:

1. _____
2. _____
3. _____

Identify alternative solutions to the #1 problem and evaluate how each one would solve the #1 problem (relate to course material where applicable):

1. _____
Evaluation: _____
_____
_____

2. _____
Evaluation: _____
_____
_____

3. _____
Evaluation: _____
_____
_____

Case Worksheet (cont'd)

Identify the most effective solution to #1 problem (relate to course material when possible):

_____

_____

_____

Defend why you chose the above as the most effective solution (relate to course material when possible):

_____

_____

_____

_____

Indicate how you would implement the most effective solution (action plan):

_____

_____

The easiest way to grade cases is to use what is called a "Case Evaluation Form." An example is shown in Chapter 14. By grading each case according to a points system you can ensure each student's work is graded fairly and in a consistent manner. This is particularly useful when cases are long and involved.

Choosing Cases: Make sure that you choose cases appropriate to the level of the material being taught. For example, when using cases in a general survey course you might want to use shorter, less complicated cases than you would use in a more focussed course. You can use cases in survey courses to illustrate particular points in a text, in essence, using the case as a mini-discussion focus point. Using longer cases in a survey course might be counterproductive because the complexity of the case (not the subject it addresses) will affect the ability of the students to tie the material in the text to the world outside the classroom. In courses where students are required to do a more in-depth analysis of the material in the text, you can use longer and more involved cases. Longer cases can also be used as a focal point of a class project.

**A
L
E
R
T**

When To Assign Cases: As mentioned in Part I of this manual, assigning cases along with the next readings from a chapter in a textbook motivates students to begin organizing the textbook material in some coherent fashion, even though you may not have covered it yet in class.

Using Role-playing

In role-playing students are given a scenario to act out. They are provided with a description of the topic, a general description of a problem situation, and a description of the particular role they are to play. This teaching technique is particularly effective in helping students understand the different positions, attitudes, concerns, or emotions people can hold about a specific topic. For example, a topic could be "giving effective feedback to an employee." The situation that addresses this topic could revolve around motivating an employee to improve his or her performance. Textbooks in disciplines like management, counseling, or education often contain sample role-plays for use in the classroom.

Role-playing in the classroom can be done either as a single or multiple task activity. In a single task role-play the instructor asks two students to conduct the role-play in front of the class while the rest of the class observes. At the completion of the role-play, the teacher conducts a general discussion of the situation and how the players behaved. The players are often asked to share their insights first and then the observers follow with their feedback. During the discussion the instructor is able to identify for the students the correct way(s) to resolve an issue or problem.

A multiple task role-play is the same as a single task role-play except all the students in the class are placed in three-person teams with one student serving as the observer. After the role-play, each group analyzes the interactions and identifies areas where they learned something important about the topic under discussion. Each group then reports to the class how it analyzed the situation and what learning took place. This format generates a more in-depth dialog because more students have an opportunity to experience the situation and to learn from closer involvement with the subject matter.

Paying careful attention to learning objectives can enhance the effectiveness of role-playing. If you don't structure the role-playing scenarios around a strong structural outline, you are depending upon students to act out a scenario in which they do not understand clearly what is expected of them. Under this set of circumstances the activity will often just fall apart or depend wholly on one student's ability to act out a particular part. To help develop strong learning objectives, you need to ask yourself before beginning to design the role-play scenarios, "What is the desired learning that needs to take place?" Once you have an answer to this question, it is relatively easy to create a realistic situation and easy-to-follow role-play directions.

Role-playing Environment: **Role-playing works best in classes where the learning environment has been one that emphasizes student participation and open discussion. Role-play will also be more successful in a class environment in which the students feel comfortable with one another and with the instructor.**

Using Review Sessions

If time allows it is always important to give students the option of meeting with you outside of class to review material they don't understand. The challenge is in finding the time and a place to do it that fits in with your schedule, as well as that of the students.

Another challenge is that you may find a particular student that asks over and over again if he or she can review something with you. You have to decide if this student really has problems understanding the material or just wants to get to know you better so you will be more lenient when grading time comes around. Don't laugh – it happens! If this is the case, you need to put a stop to this behavior in a firm yet diplomatic way.

Other Teaching Tools

We've only scratched the surface in presenting the many tools you can use to facilitate learning in the classroom. Group discussions, team debates, one-minute papers, games and simulations, and a host of other tools are also available to new teachers. See the Appendix for links to these tools.

NOTES:

_____

_____

_____

_____

_____

_____

_____

_____

_____

_____

_____

_____

_____

_____

_____

_____

_____

_____

_____

_____

_____

_____

Chapter 9

How Teachers Teach

In this chapter:

Understanding the Basics

Part-time teachers may not be as technically proficient in the classroom as their full-time counterparts, but they can be as good, if not better, at motivating students. They often have workplace experience they can use to link academic theory with real-world application. Yet, if part-time teachers don't understand some basic principles of teaching before going into the classroom environment, it can be incredibly frustrating for both the teacher and the student. This section of the manual is designed to give you some basic skills to get you successfully through your first classes.

What Your Students Want

To be an effective teacher you need to know what your students want out of your course. This changes from student to student, class to class, school to school. Student needs can include the goals you set for them in class. They can also include more basic goals such as:

✓ Just getting the course over with

✓ Learning a skill that can be used to get or keep a job

✓ "Psyching" out the teacher to find out how to get as good a grade as possible with the minimum amount of work

✓ Learning a new skill just for the sake of learning a new skill

✓ Getting the minimum passing grade with the least amount of work

✓ Getting the highest grade possible.

Students come in all shapes and sizes, with a diverse range of learning styles. Teachers often find a mixture of traditional students, nontraditional students, and foreign students in their classrooms. The part-time teacher has to be ready with a number of teaching techniques that will motivate the largest number of students in a particular class.

Many of today's students also have expectations that are different from students in earlier generations. They are more demanding and expect teachers to make the course material more relevant than just some words on the page of a textbook. They also expect the material to be presented in a more graphically enhanced manner than in the past.

Your First Class

When meeting anyone new, first impressions are critical. The classroom is no exception. You need to present yourself as a competent professional who is interested in your students not only learning the material discussed, but also understanding it in the context of how it can be used in the world outside of the classroom. Prior preparation is a must.

Looking Your Best: **You need to look your best. Particularly when teaching adult students (who may be coming from an office setting), you may need to modify the way you dress to meet the higher expectations of these working adults, at least for the first few classes. As casual dress becomes the norm in corporate America, the need to dress "up" will lessen.**

In many cases students will not have read the textbook material before the first class so you will probably be doing much of the talking during this class. Yet, you still want to set the tone for subsequent classes by encouraging two-way discussion whenever possible. The trick is to ask questions that can be answered affirmatively by students who are not yet familiar with the subject matter. Bring with you some general discussion questions that ask how the course topic might relate to the world outside the classroom. Ask for opinions. Students always have opinions, even when they might not have the right answers.

Get There Early: **Arrive at the classroom 10 to 15 minutes before the first class starts so you can greet students with a smile as they walk in. This helps the students feel more at ease right from the start. Take out your class plan and begin.**

Making introductions

Teacher's Introduction: Put your name up on the board as soon as you walk into the classroom, and put it on the board as you wish to be addressed. For example, "Mr. Winters," "Mark Winters," or "Professor Winters" (or "Dr. Winters" if the teacher has a Ph. D.) are all viable ways for Mark Winters to introduce himself to his class.

It's important that the part-time teacher does not come off as less professional than his or her full-time colleagues. Students should not be able to tell by your title or presentation style whether you are a full-time teacher or a part-time teacher. Don't make the mistake of differentiating yourself (as part-time) from your full-time colleagues. You are the teacher. No more, no less.

It's probably best to introduce yourself first and give a thumbnail sketch of your background, emphasizing the areas where it relates most closely to the class material you will be presenting. As with any introduction, keep it short.

TIP

Seating Arrangements: **Use a seating chart to help memorize the names of your students. Ask your students to stay in the same seats for the first few weeks of class so it's easier for you to put names to faces. If you have the seating chart on computer you can also use it as a roster and check off the names from the seating chart rather than a list of names on a formal roster.**

Student Introductions: The first day of class is an excellent opportunity to get to know your students better and have them get to know you better. It's also a good time to collect any information you might need from the students (email addresses, interest in the subject, experience they might have had in the subject area, etc.). You can use a student survey to accomplish this task. Refer back to Chapter 7 for more information on developing a student survey form.

If your class is small enough (20 or less) and you want to jumpstart class interaction, you can have each student introduce him or herself. In addition to their names, each one could also tell a little bit about what they do outside of the classroom and, if possible, why they are taking your class. This will help you get a better feel for the different backgrounds of the students in your class.

As people introduce themselves in smaller classes you can check them off the roster. In larger classes you will probably have to begin by calling out names from a roster. After the students have introduced themselves or you have finished calling out the roll, ask each student to introduce himself or herself to his or her neighbor. Particularly in large schools, where students are often strangers to each other, this is particularly helpful in building a healthy classroom environment. They will be spending a good part of the term with their neighbors, so they should know who their neighbors are, a little about their backgrounds, and what their majors are. You'll be surprised how the atmosphere in the class changes when the students have had a chance to introduce themselves to each other.

Ask students to put their names on a piece of paper (an 8 ½" x 11" sheet folded several times to make a triangle will usually do the trick) or a card and put it on the desk in front of them. This will make it easier to learn their names. In some schools the desks will have slots cut in them for the student to insert a nameplate.

Connecting Students: **When students are introducing themselves to one another, it's a good idea to have them trade their phone/fax/email numbers as well. This will be particularly helpful for students who might need notes for a missed class, or may need information about a project that requires input from other classmates.**

Get Those Names Right: **Using the correct pronunciation of a student's name is a good first step in building positive relationships with your students. Save yourself the embarrassment of mispronouncing someone's name by having the student say his or her name during the first roster review. Write out the difficult names phonetically so you can begin pronouncing them right from day one. Also ask the students how they want to be addressed (e.g. Mike rather than Michael) and write the revised name on your roster for future reference.**

T
I
P

Nameplate Formats: **Students seldom bring dark felt-tip markers with them to class, and if you ask them to write their names on name placards, you get all levels of readability. If you have the time it's best to produce the name placards yourself and hand them out during the second class period (you learn the name they want to be called by during the first class). Just take an 8½" by 11" piece of paper and fold it into thirds. Then print the first name and last initial (just in case you have more than one Amy, Jim, Justin, etc.) of each student on one side of the folded paper. They can then set them up on the front of their desks to help you begin remembering names. It's much easier to remember names when you don't have to squint to read the name on the placard. In addition, if the students know you took the time to write out each card they will take extra care in bringing it with them each time.**

Using the Syllabus

Now it is time to hand out the syllabus and go over it – in detail! You should have made notations on your own copy beforehand regarding the points you want to emphasize, clarify, etc. Remind the students that if they have any questions they should refer to the syllabus first, and then contact you, not vice versa. After you have reviewed each section of the syllabus, ask the students if there are any questions. Don't rush through the syllabus. The more the students understand about the class the first day, the less time will be wasted in the future by students asking questions that have already been answered in the syllabus.

Developing a Teaching Style

For many new teachers, teaching is an experience unlike any other. Many liken the experience to being an actor on a stage, with the audience being a classroom full of students. There are any number of books and articles available on how to be an effective teacher. We will cover only a few of the basics here. If you're interested in learning more about the art of teaching, please refer to the sources listed in the Appendix.

The basics

In the past, traditional teaching styles in higher education fell into two basic groups:

✓ **Teacher-centered**: strong dependence on lectures, teacher as motivator, student as participant in a teacher-led dialog. Characterized as the "sage on the stage" method.

✓ **Student-centered**: strong dependence on a student's own motivation to learn using collaborative learning, learning contracts, and independent study. Characterized as the "guide at the side" method.

Today a third classification is often used to describe a more effective way of looking at the teaching process:

✓ **Learning-centered**: strong dependence on those teaching and learning skills that are outcome oriented, skills that facilitate the learning process, no matter the method used.

Your own particular style will depend on what you're most comfortable with, how your students learn the most from you, and the type of material they need to learn. And your teaching style will evolve over time. You may start out as a motivator/lecturer and gradually include more self-directed learning tasks in your teaching style.

Many part-time teachers find their teaching technique evolves using a two-step process. Most begin using the teacher-centered method, with a heavy emphasis on "presenting material." But, as they become more comfortable with the subject matter, teachers often begin looking for ways to provide a more meaningful learning environment for their students. They will begin looking at more student-centered teaching tools and those that stress outcomes rather than techniques.

One criticism of part-time teachers is that they don't spend enough time making the classroom an active learning environment. Yet, many of your full-time colleagues face the same problem in their classrooms. Both part-time and full-time teachers need to look at teaching as a learning process for the teacher as well as the students. Teachers should be focussing on enhancing their teaching skills so they are moving away from the more traditional teacher-centered styles of teaching to a teaching style that more actively stimulates the learning process.

What's Covered? **A good way to start not only your first class presentation, but all of your presentations during the term is to review with the students what is going to be covered in class that day.**

Varying Your Presentation Style: **To facilitate the learning process, you should vary your presentation style. Studies have shown that teachers should spend only 20 to 25 minutes using a particular teaching technique before switching to another. For example, you might begin with straight lecture and move to student participation through question-and-answer discussion. It may not be feasible, but it is always helpful if you can switch tempos once or twice during each class to hold your students' interest.**

Teacher as Actor: **You are an actor on a stage, trying to hold the interest of your audience. Ensure that you project your voice so that the person in the last row can hear you. You may want to record one of your presentations (using either video or audiocassette). Then you can hear how you sound and find out how good you are at projecting your voice so all can hear. Listening to the recording will also let you know if you are putting enough inflection in your voice to hold the students' attention.**

Common Teaching Styles

The teaching styles that are discussed here are the ones commonly used by teachers in today's classrooms. In the past there was a greater emphasis put on the straight lecture method. Fortunately, this is changing as teachers move toward a more learning centered approach to teaching. There are other styles. The resources listed in the Appendix can direct you to additional teaching styles that you may also want to review.

The straight lecture method

This teaching style is used to give information to students. It is primarily one-way communication, from the teacher to the student, and is often used to support or defend information found in the text or to add additional material not covered in the text. Using real life experiences to supplement the lecture material will help make it more interesting.

Pros:

- Easy for the teacher who is not comfortable interacting with his or her students.

- Provides the opportunity to introduce information not found in the textbook or other assigned materials.

- Works for any size of class, large or small.

- Lends itself well to teachers who like to "explain" things.

Cons:

- Does not generate spontaneity among students.

- Requires that the students understand all you are saying.

- Not particularly effective as a learning technique when compared to other approaches.

- Seen as a very "controlling" style of teaching.

Changing Tempo of Lectures: **If you depend heavily on the straight lecture method, you need to change the tempo of your presentation frequently to hold interest. Using visual aids helps.**

The Importance of Good Eye Contact: **You use your voice to provide the information and you use your eyes to focus the direction the information is being delivered. Eye contact is critical in keeping the student's attention. Use frequent eye contact to show that you care about the students to whom you are speaking.**

The discussion method

The question-and-answer discussion style of teaching gets students more involved in the learning process than does the straight lecture method. It also motivates students to keep up with the material because they know they might be called on at any time to respond to a question. This style of teaching also lets the teacher know how much material students have acquired (or not acquired) through the reading of the textbook or outside material. The trick is to use questioning as positive, not negative reinforcement. If you want to generate more discussion, begin with open-ended questions like, "In your opinion, what do you think …?" or "What do you believe about this particular subject?" or "What part of that subject do you think works best?" In this way students don't start out responding to a question with a definite right or wrong answer. As the class progresses you can begin asking questions that require more specific answers.

Pros:

- Facilitates learning through active discussion.

- Students are more involved in the learning process.

- Provides immediate feedback on how well students understand the material.

Cons:

- Requires teachers to develop a questioning technique.

- Takes more class time than the straight lecture method.

- Requires that the teacher "direct" the discussion in such a way that it focuses on material relevant to the learning of the subject in question.

Responding To Student's Efforts: **Early in the term, when you are more interested in motivating students to become involved in the discussion than in getting the right answers, you might want to respond to students in the following way. When someone does not get the answer exactly right, but there is some hint of right in the answer, you might want to respond by**

saying, "That was in the right direction. Can anyone help him/her out?" Or if you think the student knows the answer, but hasn't expressed it well, you might ask, "Can you rephrase your answer?"

Address Individuals, Not the Class: If you ask "the class" a question then you spend time choosing someone to answer when the hands go up. In addition, the students who are always prepared will call out the answer and not give others in the class a chance to respond. You might want to begin the term by choosing students to respond to questions and later in the term, after students have become more comfortable with responding, move to a more open response type of questioning.

Another way to generate discussions is to use one of the following tools:

✓ Break the class up into <u>discussion groups</u> on specific topics and have each group present its consensus to the class.

✓ Set up <u>problem solving sessions</u> with group or individual work.

✓ Assign a question to a group of students and have them <u>debate</u> the pros and cons of the subject.

✓ <u>Role-play</u> the different scenarios of a problem.

Don't Get Drawn into the Lecture Trap: If you are a proponent of the question-and-answer style of teaching and find that you are lecturing more than you would like and asking questions less than you'd like, take a moment to step back and evaluate your teaching technique. Straight lecturing is easier for the inexperienced teacher than a mixture of lecture and question-and-answer discussion. It's also easy to fall back on lecturing if you are bored with the material. Look at your methodology and see where you can change it to make it more exciting for both you and the students. Add new ways of looking at old material such as using projects, debates, and in-class group work for.

Cooperative learning

This method of teaching relies on the interaction of students with other students, as well as with the teacher, to facilitate the learning process. It focuses on learning through group interaction and task management. Although students are individually accountable for their learning experience, the actual learning comes about through activities that encourage cooperative and pro-social behavior to accomplish common learning tasks.

Activities that support cooperative learning activities include roundtable discussions, role-playing , interviewing, brainstorming, "games" (e.g. marketing games), structured learning teams, and a host of other activities that involve students in the "discovery process" of learning. For more information on these learning tools, refer to the Appendix resources.

Pros:

- Actively involves the students in the learning process.

- Requires that the student do more than memorize material.

- Facilitates the longer term retention of material than other methods.

- Often requires real-world application of the material.

Cons:

- Requires that a teacher understand the many learning tools available and be able to weigh the value of each given the subject to be taught.

- Requires that the teacher develop a grading system that effectively evaluates individual learning outcomes within a team oriented learning environment.

- Requires that the teacher hand over some of the responsibility for learning to the student.

The Best Teaching Style?

There is no "best" teaching style. Some teachers do as well with straight lectures as others do with more interactive class participation. Each teacher must develop his or her own style. Much of that style will come from your own personality. Class evaluations and exams will help show you if you are doing the job or not.

 Evaluating Your Classroom Style: **Have your class videotaped so you can see how well you use gestures or how often you make eye contact with your students. It's sometimes helpful to have a professor who is known as a "good" teacher sit in your class and critique your style. Ask your department chairperson to provide you with the names of teachers who would make good (and positive) critics.**

Developing Your Teaching Style

Here are some additional points you might want to consider to increase your effectiveness as a teacher:

✓ Part-time teachers have a very special role to play in delivering a quality teaching product. You can give a lecture in which you provide information, but learning may not take place. Getting students to not only listen, but to interact in the classroom and provide you with feedback on how they see the subject at hand is where real learning takes place. You need to isolate the essence of the course material for the students and then make the course material relevant by connecting it with experience outside of the classroom (through the use of examples taken from your own work background).

✓ The more your goals and the goals of your students overlap, the more learning will take place. In order to accomplish this the teacher has to understand what motivates students (grades, knowledge, etc.) and make sure the objectives of the course address those needs whenever possible.

✓ The more you can connect the course work to experiences the students may have had in the past, the quicker students will retain the new information.

✓ One of the most difficult challenges you will face is in getting students to "unlearn" erroneous or misleading information. This is particularly true if you are teaching concepts that are a new approach to an old problem. You will first have to neutralize the impact of the knowledge already learned by the students and then begin teaching the new approach. If you don't, it will be very difficult for you to get the students to accept the new approach.

✓ If you can base your teaching on a structure that the students are familiar with, such as the outline of a textbook chapter, it will help them better organize the information in their own minds.

✓ Students need continuous feedback from the teacher on what they are learning in class. One way of doing this is to cover a subject in one class and review it at the beginning of the next class to reinforce the learning process through repetition. Being able to apply newly learned knowledge to a critical problem also provides vital feedback.

✓ Using a project as a learning tool will help students think on their own and encourage them to give themselves feedback as the project progresses.

✓ How you evaluate students can have a big impact on how they learn. Your evaluation methods must be logical, fair, and as unbiased as possible. Otherwise students will look upon the evaluation tools as unfair and respond to them (and you) accordingly.

✓ The more you believe in the ability of your students, the more they will respond in a positive way to your teaching.

✓ You will need to find a balance between challenging students to meet higher goals and supporting them should they need help in reaching those goals. This is something that comes with practice.

✓ The teaching environment is a complicated one. It needs your full attention when you are in front of your class. It's an awesome responsibility that teachers have, to teach students skills they may depend on for a livelihood once outside of the classroom.

✓ Looking for questions that encourage students to integrate materials, debate merits of concepts, and examine underlying assumptions should be one of your primary objectives as a teacher.

 The Importance of Learning Names: **Learning each student's name is not always possible, particularly with larger classes. Yet, the quicker you can learn the students' names the more connected the students will be to you, and as a result, the more motivated they will be to participate in class discussions.**

 Don't Get Too Far Off Track: **If a student asks a question that has little or no relevance to the subject matter being discussed, or would require an excessive amount of time to answer, tell the student the problem you have in answering the question at that time and that you will answer his or her question after class.**

Thinking Outside of the Box!

Teachers often run into problems when asking students to analyze a particular problem and come up with a unique or "outside of the box" solution. To the average student everything in a textbook or outside reading material is of equal importance until someone (like you) points out what is most important. They cannot make the distinction themselves because they are, in many cases, seeing the material for the first time and have little or no experience with the material outside of the academic environment. This is particularly true for full-time students just out of high school. This is where your experience "in the field" can help highlight those points that are critical to the application of the material outside of the classroom. In essence, you need to first help your students understand what a "box" looks like (society's current view of a particular subject). Only after the students understand the parameters of the box can they begin thinking outside of it.

Class Size: Is Bigger Better?

Class size pretty well dictates the amount of time you can spend on a particular classroom activity. The dynamics of classes of different sizes can vary a great deal. Your department chairperson or teachers who have taught your class in the past should be able to give you an idea of the standard class size for your course. The smaller the class, the more the interaction with and between students is possible. The larger the class, the less interaction is possible and the more important the quality of the teacher's presentation skills becomes.

Small classes

Small classes, usually 20 students or less, allow you to deliver a more personal learning experience. Night and weekend classes will tend to have a smaller numbers of students than day classes. In small classes students can better develop the analytical skills they will need when they graduate, skills like problem solving, relationship building and analytical thinking about related issues.

Teachers need facilitation skills to make teaching small classes effective. Students need motivation to prepare for small classes so they are ready for the amount of discussion small classes are best at fostering. In small classes it's also easier to learn everyone's name, which helps in building a relationship between you and the student. This often goes a long way toward reinforcing the learning process.

Moving From Large to Small Classes: **If your students are used to large, lecture-style classes where discussion is minimal and reading the assigned material before class not always necessary, they may carry these learning habits into smaller classes. You will have to work hard in the first few classes to reorient their study habits for the small class environment.**

| A |
| L |
| E |
| R |
| T |

Personality Problems: Teachers need to be ready to deal with monitoring and managing behavior in smaller classes where personalities can clash more easily and some students may try to monopolize class participation.

Large classes

Visual aids become increasingly important as class size increases. This is particularly true when making announcements about assignments not listed in the syllabus. Students will often write down what they see on an overhead where they might miss it if the instructions are just part of the instructor's lecture. In larger classes discussion groups are more effective in generating individual expression than is discussion in the larger classroom setting.

Time management becomes a bigger issue with larger classes. The teacher deals not only with having to grade a larger number of papers, giving a larger number of tests, and meeting with more students outside of class, but also has to handle the physical movement of more pieces of paper and materials in class. There will also be more questions from students about the material presented. This all takes time out of the limited time available for presentation and discussion.

With larger groups it is important that the professor has a very clear idea of what needs to be discussed during the class period. It's easy for discussions to get out of hand in large classes. Important points might be left out because of the amount of discussion time taken up by another subject. The teacher should try to stick to the timetable in the lesson plan whenever possible.

Class size will also have an effect on the type of tests that are given. Often, as class size increases, so does the use of multiple choice and true/false questions. This is not always in the best interest of the student. You can read more about this problem in the section on evaluation.

Getting Students Involved: **One way to get your students involved in the learning process is to break large classes up into smaller discussion groups that meet the last 20 minutes of the class period. Give out topics to be discussed and directions as to what they should cover in the discussion groups. Then have the groups present their discussion summaries during the last five minutes of class. To save time, one person in each group can give the group summary.**

Passing Out Papers: **Use care in passing graded papers back to students. Make sure it's the individual student's choice whether or not a classmate sees his or her grade. Some teachers fold the papers in half, length-ways, prior to class to make sure only the student whose name is on the paper sees the grade.**

Computer Help: **As class size becomes larger you should depend more on the computer to keep track of things like grades and attendance.**

As class size gets larger the time taken up passing out support material or outside reading assignments increases. If you normally hand out additional material in class, designate a corner of your desk, or a desk nearby, as the handout area. Tell students that as they come in the door before class, they are to pick up any material you have laid there before taking their seats.

When collecting an assignment you might have each student leave the assignment at their desk when they leave the class. Then you can pick them up in order, grade them in the same order, and be able to quickly pass them out during the next class because they are already in order.

If you want to collect material before the class lets out, have each student pass their assignment to the front by putting theirs on top of the student's work behind them (and only pass the pile forward when they have received the student's from behind). Then you collect it in front all in order.

Seating Arrangements

Your teaching style will be somewhat influenced by the seating arrangement of the seats in your classroom.

Traditional row and aisle seating: Many classrooms have the traditional rows of seats moving back from the front of the room. It's difficult to generate good student interaction in this kind of classroom, because, except for the front row, you are normally addressing someone over someone else's head. It's difficult to see name placards because they are often blocked from view by the student in the seat in front. One way to use this classroom arrangement effectively is to assign seats and have a seating chart so you can call on people. Before calling on a student, move down the aisle, or nearer to the student's side of the class in order to establish better eye contact.

U-shaped seating: A "U"-shaped seating arrangement, where you can walk into the open area and interact with each student, is very effective. Students can see and interact with each other as well as the teacher. This environment is also more conducive to a question-and-answer style of teaching than is the traditional seating arrangement of rows and aisles. It's also easier to see faces and read each student's name placard.

Stadium seating: Many larger schools now have the round, stadium-style seating arrangement. This is better than the traditional row and aisle arrangement because each tier is usually higher as you go back. It's easier to see nameplates and to keep good eye contact. Unfortunately, because of the tiers, it's almost impossible to roam among the students.

Requesting Seating Arrangements: **If you don't like the seating arrangement in your class, request a room with a different seating arrangement, particularly for smaller classes. It never hurts to ask.**

The Electronic Communication Revolution

The question we need to ask ourselves as teachers is not what can we do with technology, but rather what do we want to accomplish in our courses and how can we use technology to do it. Not an easy question to answer if you don't know what you want to accomplish. Once you know what you want to accomplish, ask yourself whether technology will help you or not. Teachers at many schools are asking this question right now, and there are as many answers as there are teachers asking the questions.

Teachers in today's colleges and universities have found instructional technology (IT) to be useful in three areas:

✓ Instructional technology in the classroom: to enhance the classroom learning experience.

✓ Instructional technology outside of the classroom: to augment the classroom learning experience.

✓ Instructional technology as the classroom: where the medium, the computer and the Internet, takes the place of the classroom.

Electronic communication, whether it be via the World Wide Web, email, or electronic conferencing, has a major role to play in each of these areas. The key to the effectiveness of the computer is its ability to deliver material in such a variety of ways that it can meet any number of learning styles.

Instructional technology in the classroom

Teachers with "smart classrooms" – classrooms equipped with computers, Internet connections, and multimedia projectors – have at their fingertips a magic carpet to the world outside the classroom. Through the use of the Internet, CD-ROMs and video libraries, students have an opportunity to bridge the gap between seeing something in a book and seeing it happen, sometimes even as the event is taking place. The challenge for teachers is how to use the new communication media to make teaching more effective, rather than just more entertaining. An additional challenge for teachers is whether they have the time and expertise to understand the digital medium well enough to use it effectively.

A case in point is the increasing use of presentation programs, like Microsoft's PowerPoint®, in the classroom. Many teachers have taken their notes (which in the past were written out longhand, typed up on a word processor, or put on overhead film) and have turned them into PowerPoint® presentations. This is all well and good, but many teachers have the impression that because they are now presenting the material via the computer they are providing a better learning environment. The material may be better organized and have some extra bells and whistles to give it more entertainment value, yet in most cases, all teachers have done is transfer their old teaching style (teacher-centered) from one format (written notes, overheads, etc.) to another (presentation graphics). The result is little or no additional learning benefit to the student.

In fact, using presentation software may hinder rather than enhance learning. Because presentation software often allows teachers to include more material in their lectures, the use of this presentation format increases the amount of information a student has to absorb in one sitting. In the past students had time to absorb what they were hearing as the professor wrote it on the board. Now, there is no time to think about the material as the teacher quickly flips through the presentation "slides." The challenge for teachers is to begin moving from the more teacher-centered presentation format to a student-centered learning format.

Instructional technology <u>outside</u> of the classroom

Through the use of electronic conferencing and email, students are able to extend their learning activities through self-directed searches, interactive group project work, and other learning enhancing activities. And in many cases, students can receive feedback from the teacher without having to be in a classroom. Teachers can give assignments that the students are to complete outside the classroom and return to the teacher via email a given number of days or hours before class begins. Students can use electronic chat rooms to work on projects, discuss upcoming assignments, or discuss material presented in class with other students.

How the teacher communicates electronically with students outside of the classroom will reflect the type of communication options available to them. Teachers can communicate with individual students via email (feedback on a project, areas where the student needs to do more work, setting up meeting times, discussion of a particular problem a student is having in class, etc.). However, email can become cumbersome when the amount of material is large or the same information is to be given out to all the students (e.g., syllabi, listing of changes to assignments, announcements of upcoming special events, general handouts, etc.). In this case the students need to be able to access a Web site to obtain the information. This might be the teacher's own site, or preferably, a site on the school's Web server.

Beside the enhancement of learning that can take place using electronic communication, teachers have found that the media itself helps some students do better. Students who are shy or uncomfortable expressing their feelings in class (or through one-on-one meetings with the instructor) may find electronic communication a much more comfortable way to exchange ideas. Learning is often enhanced through Web-based activities because it is student driven, rather than teacher driven. Students who need to have more information than was presented in class before they understand a particular concept can pick up this additional information without holding back their classmates.

Teachers can receive student feedback one of two ways. Synchronous feedback is feedback the teacher receives and responds to as he or she is sitting in front of the computer. Asynchronous feedback takes place when students send questions to a prearranged email address. The professor accesses the site periodically and responds to the messages on an as-needed basis.

Instructional technology *as* the classroom

Here is the brave new world of technology and higher education – distance learning. More and more schools are getting on the electronic superhighway and developing courses that are partially or totally taught via the Internet. Distance learning is shaking the foundations of academic tradition that has been in place for hundreds of years. No longer do students have to be in a classroom to learn. The Internet is the classroom. Whereas in the past the teacher was the purveyor of information, now the Internet is taking over that role. Teachers are becoming interpreters to help the students better understand the material presented on the Web. This is a big shift in emphasis for today's teachers and students.

Higher education faces some major challenges as it tackles distance learning. One is how to absorb the new medium into the existing academic setting. Can schools design distance learning courses that take advantage of the hands-on teaching experience teachers can provide while also reaping the rewards of instructional technology and self-directed learning? The jury is still out.

Another challenge facing schools regarding distance learning is who will develop the courses and who will provide them to students. You may hear your full-time colleagues talking about online course delivery and development tools like *Web CT®*, *eCollege®*, *Blackboard®*, and *TopClass®* (to name only a few) that schools purchase to help their staff develop and deliver Web-based courses. Some schools are ahead of the curve, allotting resources and manpower to develop and deliver relatively sophisticated distance learning courses. Other schools either don't have the resources, or are not ready to make the leap into cyberspace. The question arises then as to what will happen to schools that are not equipped to develop their own courses. Will there be only a small number of "grade A" course providers in the future, and will other schools be forced to use their material? A question without an answer – yet.

And finally, since the Internet is the great leveler, will it be private, non-academic organizations that will be generating the course content for future distance learning courses and not colleges and universities at all? Some experts question whether distance learning will continue to be a part of the existing college and university learning community, or whether it will develop its own cyberspace world apart from the traditional academic environment.

We've included just a small slice of some of the challenges today's colleges and universities are facing as a result of the electronic communication revolution.

 Academia and Distance Learning: **Distance Learning and its future in higher education is a touchy subject for many educators. One camp sees distance learning as a direct threat to its livelihood while another camp embraces it with open arms. As with most things, the truth is probably somewhere in between. For example, some four-year and research institutions are threatened by the concept while many community colleges see it as a great way to enhance their offerings to meet the needs of life-long learners. When broaching the subject with your full-time colleagues, you might want to find out how they view the subject before getting into the fray.**

And the future of instructional technology is?

These are early days in the transformation process and much has yet to be resolved. For example, using electronic communication as a teaching tool comes with a pretty hefty price tag, for both the schools involved, and for society as a whole. Some of these costs are:

A. The cost of upgrading classrooms to meet the needs of electronic communication.
B. The cost of ensuring that all students have the skills to access the computer and its communication tools.
C. The cost of connecting the learning public to the Internet.
D. The cost of hiring course designers who can develop effective learning platforms.

E. The cost of upgrading teacher skills in the effective use of the new electronic teaching tools.

Some quick IT tips

The computer can help you as a part-time teacher become more connected to your students by providing a communications medium that is not time dependent. Yet, if you use email to communicate with your students when not on campus, you need to control the quality and amount of feedback you receive or you could be easily inundated with information. Here are some quick tips to making the computer work for you and your students.

✓ If you want students to ask questions as they are studying, the best way is to set up a chat room on your school's Web server. In this way you won't get a flood of messages all asking the same question because students can see if a question has already been asked. Use the school's Web server and chat rooms to address issues that affect the class as a whole. If you have only email to work with and are asking your students to give you feedback, ask them to focus on certain aspects of the class presentation or outside project. Use email to discuss confidential topics with your students, but remember that email is not always confidential! Be careful what you say.

✓ If you have some information that you want to send out to all your students, use your school's Web site to distribute the information rather than email. Email can be laborious to work with when sending out the same material to a large number of students.

✓ If you assign a project or paper, consider asking your students to submit the item as an email attachment.

Web Space: **If you do decide to ask for assignments via email, remember that you may be getting these attachments in different formats (MS Word, WordPerfect, Mac based, PC based, zipped, unzipped, etc.) that will take some time to pull up on your own computer. Make sure you ask your class beforehand what systems and software they will be using to transmit information to your computer. Tell them what your**

system is and in what format you would like the material sent. And remember, you'll need some extra hard drive space to hold all this information. You might want to consider buying an additional hard drive that you can dedicate just to your class. Or consider using a zip drive on which you can store the information coming in from your students.

✓ If you're going to have to miss a class, ask your students to do a writing assignment and have them submit it as an email attachment before a certain date. In this way your students will have a deadline, and you will get the assignment knowing the date it was turned in.

✓ If you use PowerPoint® presentation slides, consider giving them out as handouts or make them available through the school's Web server. Then students can concentrate on the ideas you present rather than trying to write it all down as you present it.

✓ Many textbooks now offer CD-ROM and Internet based support material that you can use in your classroom. Make sure you check with your textbook publisher to learn what is available. New material is being developed every day. Some publishers want to be the teacher's online material developer and are developing their own course delivery software. Check it out.

✓ Here are some of the materials that you should distribute via your school's campus server, if it has one (used with permission of Dr. Peter Kauber, UNC-Greensboro):

    A. Syllabus.
    B. Course content review – extra notes, recommended exercises, hints, and suggestions.
    C. Assignment review – content required, why assigned, grading considerations, etc.
    D. Exam related info – content to be covered, number of problems, hints, etc.
    E. Calendar of events – exams, assignment due dates.
    F. Additional resources – course-related books, articles, Web sites, etc.
    G. News – new information about anything related to the course.

✔ Find out if your school has an instructional technology department and get to know some of the people who work there. You will need to call on them when you get bogged down in the details of using the computer to communicate with students. Find out what you can put on the school's Web server, if not this term, then next term.

✔ Be wary about agreeing to develop a Web-based distance learning course for your subject. The time and skills needed to develop such courses can be daunting. If you do commit to doing so (and you have your school's support of resources) make sure you understand the legal ramifications (copyright considerations, royalties, etc.) of building a course that can be used by more than just your school.

✔ Remember that at least for the foreseeable future, the Internet is not a replacement for face-to-face interaction with students. Meaningful "distance discussion" is still a challenge for most courseware packages. For example, some students need to hear other questions asked by fellow students before they even realize they have their own questions on the subject.

✔ Band width (which controls the amount of digital information that can be sent to a computer at one time) is not developed to the point that Web images can be downloaded or streamed at a speed that makes them as lifelike as video images. That technology is in the works, but it's not there yet.

✔ Check with your school to see if there is any legal problem in answering a student's question in a chat room and referring to that student by name.

✔ The nice thing about threaded discussion groups (chat room interchange between professor and students) is that it can be archived and saved for future reference.

✔ If you ask for homework to be turned in via email, make sure you tell your students you want it posted by a specific time before class starts (for example, two hours). This will ensure that students are taking the time to think about what they are writing and not just cramming a writing assignment into the last 30 minutes before class. Asking students to sit down in front of a computer forces them to give some thought to what they are doing.

Using Your Laptop: **If your school encourages the use of computer-assisted material in the classroom, it would be to a teacher's benefit to invest in a laptop. The teacher can store all presentation material to be used over the course of the term and have it at his or her fingertips.**

Notes On Web: **In order to have a class's undivided attention during the class discussions, some teachers put their notes out the school's Web server prior to class. This is done so students can participate in the class discussions and not spend class time simply taking notes.**

Always Test Compatibility Beforehand: **If you have your own laptop and plan to use your school's projection equipment, make sure you test the equipment with your computer before your first class. You want to ensure that your laptop can communicate with the model and settings of the projection equipment provided in the classroom.**

We hope this taste of what is coming helps you decide how you might use the new instructional technology environment to enhance your own teaching. There are any number of Web sites you can go to for more information about the subject (see Appendix). Magazines like *Syllabus* and *T.H.E. Journal* also commit a good amount of space to discussing instructional technology and the electronic communication revolution in higher education, as does *The Chronicle of Higher Education.* For additional information, see the Appendix.

NOTES:

_____

_____

_____

_____

Chapter 10

Teaching and Learning Tools

In this chapter:

Seeing and Doing

Seeing and doing are the first steps to learning. Each alone won't do the job effectively, but together they will double the chances that students will retain what you present. The teaching tools we are about to discuss will help make your classroom a more effective learning environment.

Using Overheads

With overhead transparencies you can quickly convey information to your class without having to take the time to write down the information on the board. You can also use overheads to structure your lecture, presentations, and discussions. Traditional overhead transparency projectors also let you present information to your class without having to turn your back to the class, as you do when using the board.

Control the flow: Students have a tendency to want to copy everything they see on the screen first and then refocus on the class discussion. Prevent students from writing ahead of the discussion by covering your overhead with a piece of paper and uncover the subjects to be discussed one at a time, discussing each one as you go along.

Face the audience: Make sure you spend most of your time talking to the class and not to the overhead transparency. Many teachers find their attention drawn to the bright surface of the equipment, and they forget about the class "out beyond the light."

Using Electronic Imaging Equipment

Using electronic imaging equipment requires skills similar to those needed to use overheads, but with some important differences. In some cases the projector will not be facing the audience, but will be placed against a wall or near a video system wiring jack. Therefore, you need to make sure that once your object (film, picture, text, or 3-D object) is placed on the equipment, that you look back to your audience when speaking. Because the screen can be positioned at any angle to the projecting surface, you will also have to get used to the sensation of pointing to an object on the projection surface and having your movements shown at what is seemingly an odd angle to the screen. It will take some time to get used to the system, but once you do, you will enjoy the flexibility this type of equipment gives you.

Using Videos

Videos can also be a good learning tool, but you need to be aware of both the positive and negative aspects of using videos before deciding whether to use them in your class.

The **positive** reasons for using videos include:

✓ Bringing the real world into the classroom.

✓ Strong visual stimulation for the TV and Internet generation.

✓ Can be used to fill in when there is not enough material to cover in class.

✓ Can introduce or wrap up a particular subject by showing actual application of the concepts learned in class.

The **negative** aspects of using videos include:

✓ Difficult to control video content.

✓ May not fit into time constraints.

✓ May be looked upon by students as entertainment rather than a serious learning experience.

✓ Takes time to set up before use.

✓ Video equipment may have to be scheduled ahead of time.

A teacher needs to review video content carefully to ensure that the content meets the class needs and time constraints.

Using Slides

As mentioned earlier in this manual, the use of slides is being quickly overtaken today by transparencies and computer generated images. Therefore, we will not discuss slides in any more detail. Suffice it to say that lighting (or absence of) is the major problem when using slide projectors to project images onto a screen. In most cases, the classroom lights have to be off and window blinds drawn. Students can only watch, but are precluded from taking notes because of the lack of light. One solution to this problem is to have the slides scanned and made into overheads or PowerPoint® slides.

Using Blackboards and Whiteboards

Using a black, green, or white board is still a mainstay in today's classroom. If used effectively they can be very useful tools. If not used effectively, their use can be seen as just so much gibberish thrown up on a board.

Here are some tips for using a board, whether it is a black (or green) board that requires you to use chalk or a white board on which you use erasable felt-tip markers.

Talking and writing: Don't talk and write at the same time. It may be difficult for the students to hear you when you are talking into the board. When speaking, face the students. If you feel you must talk while writing, raise your voice so you can be heard.

Don't be a wall: Step away from the board when you're done writing to let the students see what you have written.

Erase those boards: Make sure the board is clean before you begin. Knock the erasers on the end of the eraser tray before cleaning to knock excess chalk or marker "dust" from the eraser. Vertical downward strokes of the eraser will clean a blackboard better then horizontal strokes, which only moves the chalk around rather than depositing it in the eraser tray below.

Posture: If you want to ensure that your sentences don't run downhill as you move across the board, face the board squarely as you write.

"Keep It Simple" format is best: Rather than writing out long complex sentences, use sentence fragments to support key points.

Colors: When using blackboards, yellow or white chalk is best. Other colors are difficult to see from a distance. When using whiteboards, most colors work, although the darker colors (black, green, and blue) are easier to read from a distance.

Pause for effect: Don't erase the board too soon. Always let students finish copying down the material you have put on the board before erasing it or moving on to a new topic.

 ***Walk Back and Look at Your Board:* You should take a moment during the first few classes to walk to the back of the room and look at the board as if you were a student. You can then tell how legible your writing is and notice areas where you might want to improve your board techniques.**

Using the Computer

Although the impact of the computer on today's classrooms was covered in the last chapter, a few points should be made about the basic skills you will need to be effective in the "wired" classroom. Computer presentations using software programs like PowerPoint® and similar software are becoming commonplace in today's classrooms. Publishers are making more and more computer-generated material available as part of the teacher's textbook package. Some universities and colleges are now requiring that students carry laptop computers as their predecessors once carried calculators. If you plan to use computer equipment in the classroom, make sure you are familiar with the particular equipment available and how to access it during class (e.g., how to unlock computer cabinets, turn on power strips, etc.).

Your full-time colleagues may be putting some of their class materials on the school's Web server and asking students to download the information for their own reference (e.g. syllabi).

For nontraditional students this can be a problem because they come to class with varying degrees of computer experience. Some may have no experience at all. Nor are many of these nontraditional students on campus long enough to access the school's network. For these students it may be better to provide the materials in hardcopy form.

At a minimum, today's teachers should know how to use basic word processing, spread sheet, and presentation software. The challenge for the part-time teacher is where to find the time to learn and use this software in developing classroom presentations. Even developing simple PowerPoint® presentations can be relatively time consuming. As with everything else in teaching, it will be up to you to determine how much multimedia material you want to develop for your class, and to find the resources at your school to develop the material.

Using Projection Screens

Projection screens come in all shapes and sizes: floor mounted, wall mounted, ceiling mounted and portable. Some extend simply by touching a button on the wall. Others take several minutes to set up. If the handle on a ceiling mounted screen is located above the average teacher's reach, there is usually a stick with a hook in it standing nearby to bring the screen down. Before you begin class make sure that stick hasn't walked off.

Some modern pull-down screens have a locking device in the handle that lets you lock it in place when the screen is fully extended. To unlock the screen you twist the handle and then let the screen roll up. Take some time to practice using the screen controls in your classroom before class begins.

Using the Textbook

Today's textbooks are a far cry from those of just ten years ago. Long the mainstay of the traditional classroom, the textbook is just beginning to feel the effects of the electronic media on its dominance. Most use four-color photos and artwork to illustrate the subject matter. In the last several years textbook authors have been adding Internet site references to their books as well as setting up Web sites to answer questions, add updates to the texts, and gather information for future editions.

In many cases students still depend on the textbook as their primary information resource. Teachers will find that if they can use the textbook to provide the structure around which their courses are built, it will help students organize their own study habits and help them keep up with additional information as it is presented in class.

Ideally your job is to help students understand the material in the textbook by acting as a bridge between the material in the book and the world outside the classroom. The students' task is to be sure they understand the material in the text and come to you if they have any questions.

NOTES:

Part IV

Evaluating Students

Chapter 11

Grading and Evaluation

In this chapter:

The Really Tough Bit

It must be said up front that evaluating students is not, as much as we would like to think otherwise, a question of absolutes. There are shades of gray in the grading process just as there are in any other aspect of the teaching profession. You will have some good students, and you will have some who are not so good. It's your job to evaluate your students fairly and impartially by the work they do in an imperfect world.

For the new teacher, evaluating student performance can be the most difficult part of the teaching process. During the evaluation process you may be taking into consideration variables like: Is the student a traditional or nontraditional student? Does the student work full-time as well as go to school? Does the student's company only pay for the course if the student makes a B or above? Yet, at the end of the day there must be a direct relationship between what you teach and what you test for. What you emphasize in class and in work done outside of class for your course should be the major focus of your evaluation efforts. Everything else, while having some impact, should not play a major role in the evaluation process.

Grade Inflation

Prior to the 1980s it was not uncommon for undergraduate students to get C's and accept it as a matter of course. It was understood at the time that a C was a grade for average work. Not bad work, but not exemplary, either. It was meeting the basic requirements of the course. Today many undergraduate students believe getting a C is the same as failing. Now many students believe a B to be the norm, whereas in the past it was a reward for doing better than expected. And today, good students expect A's, although in the past it was only the very best students who received an A grade. If you are just getting into teaching, this will be something you need to take into consideration when evaluating students.

We tell you this not to encourage you to compromise your values and inflate your grades to meet these expectations, but that you should be aware of these expectations when you start the evaluation process. This is one of the reasons it is important for you to get an idea from your department head of past grades given out in your course (or related courses) and what your school's expectations are (if any) regarding grading for your course. There will be a lot of pressure on you from students for B's and A's, particularly from students who feel the pressure to earn the grades they feel they need to get into graduate school.

On the other side of the ledger are teachers who believe giving high grades is a mark of a teacher who is not tough enough. This is the other side of the coin and is just as unrealistic.

***Documentation:* It is important that you carefully document your evaluation process and be ready to explain your grading system to any concerned student or administrator who wants to see it. It must therefore be fair and consistent. There will always be some students who do not agree with the grade you have given them and will come back after the end of the school term and argue for a better grade. Here is where it is important that you have a well documented and fair grading system to show students why they received the grade they did.**

***Grades Get Better:* Juniors and seniors should, by nature, have slightly better grades than their freshman and sophomore colleagues because of the weeding-out process that takes place as students progress through the grade levels. You can also expect higher grades in elective classes because students have chosen these classes out of interest, not because they have been forced to take them as a required course.**

Elements of Good Grading

For the final grade to be an effective mirror of a student's efforts over the school term, you need to ensure that the evaluation methods are:

✓ **Valid** – They measure what they are supposed to measure (for example, course objectives).

✓ **Reliable** – They produce similar results on a consistent basis, test after test, student after student.

✓ **Comprehensive** – They test a representative amount of the material covered in the course.

✓ **Practical** – They are practical to design and administer, given the time and resources available.

✓ **Consistent** – They use the same style of wording you used when the material was presented during class discussion.

✓ **Understood** – Students clearly understand how their work will be evaluated. This includes instructions for the evaluation tools that are clear and complete.

Understanding the Process: **The element of good grading that is the most overlooked, and at the same time the key to the process, is that the grading system is understood by the students. You can have the best, most reliable system in the world, but if your students can't understand the process and what they need to do to make the grade, you've wasted a lot of your (and your students') valuable time.**

Different Grading Tools

The first step in the evaluation process is to use tools that will give you a realistic evaluation of the student's efforts over the term. These tools include:

✓ Tests and quizzes

✓ Class participation

✓ Homework

✓ Writing assignments/papers

✓ Projects

✓ Case evaluation and analysis

✓ Lab work

Depending on the subject area, there are other more specialized forms of evaluation tools. In this manual we review only the ones listed above, as they will cover many of your evaluation needs.

NOTE: We use the word "test" to denote several different evaluation tools, which can include exams, midterms, finals, and quizzes. If there is a need to differentiate the kind of test we are talking about as we go along, we will do so.

Multiple Evaluation Tools: **You will get a more accurate evaluation of student learning by using multiple evaluation tools in a course. This approach is also sensitive to the diversity among students' learning styles and needs.**

Different Grading Systems

There are as many grading systems as there are teaching styles. No matter which system you use, it is important that your grading is consistent, understandable, and conducive to helping both you and your students meet the goals and objectives of the course.

It bears repeating that it's important that you find out if your department has a list of departmental policies and/or conventions you need to follow in your evaluation process. Your school may require that you use a particular grading system. They may also be able to provide a printout of the average grades students normally make in your course or courses similar to it. You can use these as guides when developing your own grading policy.

Two of the most common grading systems are the "relative" grading system and the "absolute" grading system.

Relative grading system: Using this system a teacher evaluates the performance of each student against the other students in the same class. Grades are awarded on the basis of where a student's score falls among all the scores *in that particular class*, and no other. The objective is to grade along a bell-shaped or normal distribution curve in which there are some A's and some F's (at both ends of the curve) and the majority of the students fall somewhere in between the two extremes with B's, C's, and D's.

One way to grade students using the relative grading system is to find "natural" breaks where grades tend to separate into groups. In the example below there is a natural break between 92 and 89 and between 82 and 76. Therefore, all grades 92 and above could be A's, between 82 and 89 Bs, between 73 and 76, Cs, and so on.

Test Scores
95, 95, 94, 92, 89, 89, 87, 86, 85, 83, 82, 82, 76, 75, 74, 73, 73

Another way to grade using the relative grading system is to apportion the percentage of grades for a particular class. For example, you might give A's to the students who are in the top 10% of the class, B's for students in the top 11% to 30% of the class, Cs for students in the range of 31% to 70%, D's from 71% to 90%, and the remaining students in the range from 91% to 100% would receive an F, or failing grade. When using the relative grading method there will always be some students who make F's and some who make A's, no matter what the general level of the class is as a whole.

The ideal relative grading system is one in which all the grades of the students in a particular class are listed from lowest to highest. The median or middle score is then determined and a breakdown of scores is made according to standard deviations up or down from this middle score.

The major disadvantage of this method is that a student's final grade depends heavily on the grades of other students in the same class. Grading standards will tend to fluctuate with the general quality of each class of students. It is therefore difficult to compare classes from term to term using this method because of the differences in the quality of the students from term to term. One type of relative grading is grading "on a curve" in which a grading scale is adjusted to ensure that more students fall within a certain grade range than would have before the adjustment. We will discuss curving later on in this chapter.

EXAMPLE: Relative grading system

Assume that the point spread at the end of the term is as follows:

Alan	=	87	Jian	=	82
Beth	=	85	Klaus	=	77
Seila	=	84	Terry	=	75
Ellen	=	83	Cary	=	69
Bill	=	83	Sarah	=	68

If you used the percentage breakdown above (top 1% to 10 % get A's, the next 11% to 30% B's, etc.) the final grade distribution would be:

1 A (Alan)
2 B (Beth and Seila)
4 C (Ellen, Bill, Jian, and Klaus)
2 D (Terry and Cary)
1 F (Sarah)

As you might guess, with small classes a normal bell-shaped distribution of grades is not always possible. This is particularly true for classes that fill a special niche or classes that people have chosen because of a special interest in the subject matter. The larger the number of students in a class, the more scores will approach a normal distribution of A's, B's, C's, D's, and F's over a given population of students.

Absolute grading system: In this system students are rated against clearly established objectives that are established before the course begins. The focus is on achieving course objectives. Therefore, when determining the final grades for a class of high achievers, you could have a proportionately higher percentage of people getting good grades than you would with a class of low achievers. The challenge for both new and experienced teachers is to define reasonable objectives with which to measure a student's performance.

Below are the questions a teacher using the absolute grading system needs to ask after grading is completed:

- Did the students demonstrate an understanding of the course material as presented (and did the teacher do his or her job in presenting the material in a way that the students could understand and use it)?

- Did the students achieve the learning goals as set out in the course objectives?

- If grades were not evenly distributed, can the teacher explain why (a large number of exceptional students, poorly performing students, undo influence from activities outside the classroom, poor test questions, etc.)?

- Were the teacher's objectives reasonable given the ability of the student population as a whole?

EXAMPLE: Absolute grading system

Using an absolute grading system, a professor may decide that all students who have 90% or above of the total available points (for example, 100 points) are to receive an A. Those in the 80% to 89% percentile a B, in the 70% to 79% percentile a C, the 60% to 69% a D, and below 60%, an F. Using the same points spread given in the relative grading system example, there would be:

> **0 A**
> **6 B (Alan, Beth, Seilia, Ellen, Bill, Jian)**
> **2 C (Klaus, Terry)**
> **2 D (Cary, Sarah)**
> **0 F**

Which system works best?

Some teachers prefer the relative grading system while others prefer the absolute grading system. And many teachers use a hybrid of the two systems. For example, teachers may determine a final grade list using the absolute grading system and then adjust that list by curving the grades to come up with a more favorable (to the student) grade distribution. One advantage of the absolute grading system is that it gives students a clear indication of how well they are doing at any point throughout the term. With the relative grading system, a student does not know how much the grades of other students in the class will affect his or her grade until the grades are distributed.

Check Past Averages: Whether you use the absolute or relative grading system you should always check past average class scores to determine the grade range you should be targeting with your own grading method. Your department head should be able to provide this information.

Grading techniques

There are several techniques you can use to arrive at a final point rating for each student. Using this point rating you can decide whether to use the relative grading system or the absolute grading system to determine the final grade. These techniques are:

✔ The weighted grading method

✔ The straight-line grading method

✔ The hybrid grading method.

The weighted grading method: Using this method a teacher gives each evaluation tool (exams, projects, homework, class participation, etc.) a point value of 100 points each. Then each tool is given a weighted value in percent terms which tells the students how much weight that particular tool is given in determining the final grade. The weighted values of all the evaluation tools should equal 100%.

For example, a mid-term exam might be worth 100 points, but make up only 15% of the final grade, while a participation grade might also be worth 100 points, yet make up 40% of the final grade.

Below is an example of a weighted grading method of determining point values:

Activity	Value	Weight	Max Value
Exam 1	100 points	15%	15 points
Exam 2	100 points	15%	15 points
Participation	100 points	40%	40 points
Final Exam	100 points	30%	30 points
TOTAL	**400 points**	100%	100 points

Straight-line grading method: Using this method, a teacher gives each activity the same point value and determines the final grade by adding up each student's points from each activity. The teacher then applies the absolute or relative grading system to come up with a final grade. Below is an example of the straight-line grading method of determining point values:

Activity	Value	Weight
Exam 1	100 points	None
Exam 2	100 points	None
Participation	100 points	None
Final Exam	100 points	None
TOTAL	400 points	

Hybrid grading method: This method uses a mixture of the weighted and straight-line methods in which a teacher gives each activity a different point value depending on how much weight that particular tool is given in determining the final grade. The teacher then calculates the final points total by adding up each student's points from each activity. The weighting is already figured into the points value and doesn't need to be calculated separately.

Below is an example of the hybrid grading method of determining the final points value.

Activity	Value	Weight
Exam 1	100 points	Point values
Exam 2	100 points	Point values
Participation	300 points	Point values
Final Exam	200 points	Point values
TOTAL	700 points	

The challenge in using this style of grading is that each evaluation tool must be constructed to meet the point value assigned. For example, the final exam must be worth 200 points. If the value of test questions or homework questions does not add up to the point total in the evaluation table in your syllabus, you will have to adjust the point values so that they do. Each test or piece of homework can be multiplied by a set value to get a final point total. For example, the final exam might have 50 questions with a value of two points per question, for a total of 100 points. Yet, the final point value in the syllabus is 200. You would need to let your students know when test time comes around that you will be multiplying their grade (maximum 2 x 50 or 100) by 2 to come up with the weighted value in the syllabus (200). Most teachers find it's much simpler just to make the point values on the test add up to the weighted value of the grade. In the above example, each test question would be worth 4 points rather than 2, for a total of 200.

Weighted, straight-line, or hybrid?

It depends on how easy you want to make it for your students to evaluate their progress as the class progresses. For example, the weighted grading method is more difficult to use then the straight-line and hybrid methods because more complex calculations have to be done to come up with the numerical point total.

Putting it together

There is not enough space here to provide an example of every iteration of the grading systems described above. Yet, to give you an idea of what the final product might look like, we'll choose one grading system and one method of determining the final point value as an example.

If for example you decided to follow the *absolute grading system* and use the *hybrid grading method* to generate point totals, the results might look as follows:

Hybrid + Absolute

Activity	Value	Grade	Scale	
Exam 1	100 points	A	= 630-700	(90%-100%)
Exam 2	100 points	B	= 560-629	(80%-89%)
Participation	300 points	C	= 490-559	(70%-79%)
Final Exam	200 points	D	= 420-489	(60%-69%)
TOTAL	**700 points**	F	= 0-419	(< 60%)

In this example, any student whose final grade is between 630 and 700 will get an A. Those whose final grade is between 560 and 629, a B, and so on.

Grading on a curve

Even if you suspect that at the end of the school term you will have to grade on a curve (adjusting the class' grades upward in order to raise the overall level of the class average), it's not wise to indicate it in the syllabus or verbally to your students. Students are less motivated if they know a teacher regularly grades on a curve. If you are asked if you grade on a curve, reserve the right to make that decision later in the term by indicating you normally do not grade on a curve or that you only grade on a curve under extenuating circumstances. Yet, if you never grade on a curve, state it very clearly in the syllabus so there are no surprises at the end of the term for students who might have thought otherwise.

As a new teacher you may find you must grade on a curve the first term or two to compensate for problems you may have had in test design, project evaluation, and everything else that goes along with being a new teacher. You might want to ask if your department has a policy on curving before proceeding.

The Bottom Line

Assigning final grades ranks right up there with root canal work for pain and frustration. It can be one of the most difficult tasks you will ever undertake as a teacher. It involves the use of many different evaluation skills, both objective and subjective. The final grade should be the result of a relatively equal spread of activities (exams, quizzes, projects, etc.) to meet the diversity of student learning styles. It would not be fair to base 90 percent of a final grade on only one activity, such as a final exam.

The Grade Assignment Process

The final grading system you use will probably be one that falls somewhere between the absolute and relative grading systems described earlier. Much will depend on your experience in evaluation, as well as the general level of the class you are evaluating. In most cases the grading process is one of:

✓ Reviewing the status of the class:

- What type of student is being evaluated, for example, traditional or nontraditional?

- What is the general skill level of the class as a whole?

- How well were the students able to understand the concepts presented in class?

✓ Looking at the distribution of final grades after having added up all the points that a particular student earns during a term.

✓ Determining what you feel the final distribution of grades should be compared with what the actual distribution is, and then deciding how to come up with a fair grading scale using your intuition as a guide.

This is where the soul searching begins. To help make the process easier you first need to develop a spreadsheet. It might look like the one below. Notice that all categories have number ratings. Some teachers might think it more realistic to rate items like class participation with good, fair, and poor ratings. Teachers should still translate the good to poor ratings into a number grade (e.g., Good = 95, Fair = 80, Poor = 65, etc.) so that a ratings spread sheet gives them a quantifiable evaluation of what each student has accomplished.

EXAMPLE: Grading scale for Alan's class (see earlier example)

Activity		Total Points
Exam 1	=	100 pts.
Exam 2	=	100 pts.
Final Exam	=	100 pts.
Project	=	100 pts.
Class Participation	=	100 pts.
Total Possible Points =		500 pts.

Grading Scale
A = 450-500
B = 400-449
C = 350-399
D = 300-349
F = 0-299

EXAMPLE: Points earned by Alan

Activity		Total Points
Exam 1	=	100 pts.
Exam 2	=	97 pts.
Final Exam	=	87 pts.
Project	=	90 pts.
Class Participation	=	70 pts.
Total Possible Points =		444 pts.

Grading Scale
A = 450-500
B = 400-449
C = 350-399
D = 300-349
F = 0-299

Alan's final grade, using the grading scale for Alan's class, is a B (444 falls within the range 400 to 449).

Let's assume that the final point grades of Alan and his classmates are as follows (using an Excel® spreadsheet):

	A	Exam 1	Exam 2	Final Exam	Project	Class Part.	POINTS	Grd.
2	Alan	100	97	87	90	70	444	B
3	Klaus	72	78	77	76	80	383	C
4	Cary	60	65	69	75	90	359	C
5	Ellen	92	94	83	90	80	439	B
6	Beth	87	83	85	80	90	425	B
7	Jian	53	79	82	78	90	382	C
8	TOT	464	496	483	489	500	2432	

Adjusting grades

The grades in the example on the previous page are based on an absolute grading scale without any adjustment or curving. Now let's review the grades to see where we might want to adjust the grading scale to more closely reflect the class' actual performance for a specific term.

Using the example above, it looks as if Alan did very well on the tests and project, but his final point grade was strongly influenced by his poor class participation. Knowing the student, you may feel that the poor class participation grade was a result of his particular personality (shy) and not an unwillingness to work hard. Since his final point total was only 6 points away from an A, you may decide to add 6 points to everyone's total score (not just Alan's). Yet, you would only do this if it does not adversely affect what you thought was a fair distribution for all of the students that term (this is where using a spreadsheet program like Microsoft Excel ® comes in very handy to do the "what if" work).

In looking over the grade distribution you decide it would also be nice to give Jian a B as it was only his first test that held him back, and you know he has worked hard to recover from that low score. You could therefore add more points to everyone's total, but to change Jian's grade to a B would require you to adjust up all scores by 18 points. This would affect the other students' grades and increase the total grade point average of the class. Cary, who is clearly a C level student, would get a B. But it would help Klaus, who is a borderline A student with average class participation, move up into the A range.

Let's suppose you first added 6 points to the total actual points, and then looked at the grade layout and found that it was not enough. Then you added 18 points to everyone's score and went through the same review process. The final outcome would look like the following:

	Grade	GPA	Plus 6	Grade	GPA	Plus 18	Grade	GPA
Alan	B	3	450	A	4	462	A	4
Klaus	C	2	389	C	2	401	B	3
Cary	C	2	365	C	2	377	C	2
Ellen	B	3	445	B	3	457	A	4
Beth	B	3	431	B	3	443	B	3
Jian	C	2	388	C	2	400	B	3
		2.50			2.67			3.17

Notice that the original grade point average was 2.50. Adding 6 points to everyone's score brings that average up to 2.67. Adding 18 points to everyone's original score brings the average up to 3.17. Which average is the right average? It's really your call and depends to a great extent on how well you have been able to evaluate each student's performance over the course of the term.

As much as we like to be absolutely impartial, there are times when adjustments may be necessary, and the example above is one way to adjust the grading scale fairly. Yet, you must always weigh the particular character of each class with the need to remain within any average final grade guidelines for your class.

To Curve or Not To Curve: **One of the first questions you will be asked in class is, "Do you curve?" As cautioned earlier, it is unwise to let students know you curve grades. In theory, courses should be structured so you don't need to curve grades. Curving should only be used to address small variances in your class from term to term, but it should not be the primary factor on which you evaluate your students. If it is, it could mean you are asking too much of your class or not enough of yourself. On the other hand, if you curve a lot you could get a reputation for handing out easy grades. Excessive curving is a good way to fill classes, but a poor way to evaluate and reward scholastic excellence.**

Backup Copies: **Although recording grades on a computer spreadsheet can save you time in the long run, it's important that you always make a hard copy of the grades before leaving your spreadsheet program. There is nothing worse than having your computer hard drive go out and all the individual grading records you have stored up over the term get lost as well. This is particularly true if you have already given back the tests and quizzes to the students.**

Turning in Grades

Your school will probably be giving you a very specific time limit by which you have to have grades in to the school administration after the final exam. For example, 48 hours after the students take the final exam. This gives the registrar's office enough time to register the grades and send them out to students on a timely basis. One exception to this might be grades required for graduating seniors. Graduation could be scheduled only a few days after the final exam, and therefore you may be required to have senior grades in to the registrar's office even sooner than expected. Ask your department head or mentor what the policy is at your school.

NOTES:

Chapter 12

Which Tests?

In this chapter:

Why Test?

A well-written test should accomplish two things:

- Find out how well students have learned and understood the course material.

- Find out how well the teacher has been able to facilitate the learning process.

Tests are not just something you give your students so they can get a grade at the end of the term. Tests are tools that evaluate both the teacher and the student. If you are not doing a good job in helping students learn and understand the material, a well-written test will let you know your deficiencies fairly quickly.

Let's assume you're doing a pretty good job in the classroom. So, how can you use tests to show how well your students have understood the material? First, all the material in the book, in outside readings, or in your lectures is not of equal importance. As a teacher you need to let students know which concepts will be most important to them as they begin to apply what they have learned in the classroom to the world outside the classroom. One way of doing this is to always test for what you feel are the key points regarding a particular subject, not the nitpicking details. In this way you help the student sort out the wheat from the chaff by making it clear, through your tests, what is important for them to understand. This is why you need to have clear course goals and objectives in mind when developing any kind of testing tool.

What Are You Testing For?

Besides having specific course-related goals and objectives in mind before beginning to develop a test, you have to decide what the test will evaluate. Are you evaluating how well students were able to analyze a problem, how well they memorized a certain passage or set of facts, how well they understood some basic concepts, or how well they performed a certain task? Answers to these questions will influence how you will design your tests.

Which Test?

Let's review the types of testing tools available to you. The ones you choose will depend to a great extent on the learning skills you are testing for as well as the particular subject matter you are testing on.

Essay

Pro:

- Lets students respond beyond the minimum amount of response required.

- Gives an in-depth look at a student's overall ability.

- Easy to develop.

- Can be easily modified from class to class.

- Can be used to test analytic capabilities as well as memorization capabilities.

- Helps students pull concepts together into a more understandable whole.

- Good at testing depth of understanding, rather than breadth of understanding.

Con:

- Difficult to use when you want to cover a large amount of class material. For example, ten different multiple-choice questions could be answered in the same amount of time it would take a student to answer one essay question.

- Essay questions can be open to subjective evaluation. Some students are just better writers than others. It takes time and experience to develop a fair and consistent grading system for this type of question.

- Can take a long time to grade.

- Can be time consuming for students to answer, even for narrowly structured questions.

Bonus Essay Questions: Essays work particularly well as bonus questions. You can assign points to a bonus essay question or leave it open and decide how many points to assign to a bonus question after you have had a chance to grade the rest of the test. This will give you a chance to see if the bonus question has in fact generated "bonus level" thinking or not.

How long?

If you use essay questions, it's probably best to use several questions requiring shorter answers rather than one question which requires a long, involved answer. Or, narrow the focus of the longer questions to keep the answer length to a minimum. This will give a better overall testing sample of the course material.

To ask more than a few in-depth essay questions requiring lengthy responses during a 50-minute test period may be unrealistic. You have to be very specific in your own mind as to the depth of the questions you plan to ask and the time you expect it to take to answer the question. Otherwise you will have a lot of people still writing when the class ends.

For example:

An essay question that asks for a long, unfocussed answer:

Compare and contrast the work of William Shakespeare with that of Ben Jonson.

An essay question that asks for a short, focussed answer:

Describe in a half page or less three major differences between the works of William Shakespeare and Ben Jonson.

Indicate Level of Precision: **If you are asking for a numerical answer on your test, you should always indicate how precise you want the answer to be (for example, two places to the right of the decimal point). You want to let your students know how far you want them to take the problem-solving process.**

Asking for Opinions: **When using essay questions, do not ask for a student's opinion without giving some guidelines as to the type of response you are looking for. Without guidelines every student would theoretically get a perfect score, no matter what they wrote (because you are asking for their "opinion," rather than for actual facts).**

Grading essay tests

The best way to grade an essay test is to first write down the main objectives you are testing for and then compare these to what the student actually wrote.

Before grading the essay you need to decide:

1. What points are the most critical (rank as #1's)

2. What points are acceptable (rank as #2's).

If you have the time, you can check off the points in each student's essays as #1's or #2's and weigh the final grade using a ranking system with #2 points having half the value of #1 points. You can mark the papers using a single checkmark to indicate a #1 point and two checkmarks (or a circle or asterisk, etc.) to indicate a #2 point. Make sure you include in your #1 rankings any higher level skills (analytical, diagnostic, reflective) demonstrated by a student that you feel warrants extra recognition.

For example, a student's grading checklist for a question might be based on the following evaluation system:

#1 point referenced 3 times = 3 points (each point x 100%)

#2 point referenced 4 times = 2 points (each point x 50%)

Total points for question = 5

Grading Grammar and Content: Check with your department head to see if there is a departmental policy requiring you to evaluate grammar when grading any material written by students. If not, it's up to you and the type of subject you are teaching. Even if there is not a policy requiring you to grade grammar, if good grammar will be a part of how a student is evaluated in the outside world (business, journalism, etc.), you may want to grade the grammar, time allowing. Of course, when evaluating a student's work, you should also be looking for how well the student organizes his or her ideas and translates these ideas into a well-developed, well-written and concise response. If you grade the grammar as well as the material you are testing for, make sure you let your students know before the test begins.

T I P

Using a Model: **If you have time, write out the answers to the essay questions on your first test and pass them out when you hand the graded tests back. This will give your students an idea of the type and depth of response(s) you are looking for when you ask an essay question on future tests.**

A L E R T

Let Students Know How You Grade Essays: **You will find that students feel they should get all the points on an essay test, no matter how vague their answers. One way to avoid this problem is to hand out your grading criterion before the first exam. This dispels any concerns students might have about subjectivity because it will show them that you are using an objective evaluation technique. Another way to "ease their pain" is to make up several essay questions and answer them yourself. Then, well before the exam, hand your questions and corresponding answers out to the class. This will give the students a general idea of the type of response you expect on an essay test.**

Different Answers: **Be open to accepting a response that answers the question, even though you may not have considered that answer yourself.**

True/False

Because there are only two possible responses to a true/false question, students have a 50/50 chance of guessing correctly if they don't know the answer. This encourages guessing. Plus, there is a real skill to developing a true/false question where the answer is really always true or always false. The real plus for using true/false questions is that they are easy to score. True/false questions are, for the most part, not the most valid or reliable question form available to you.

Multiple Choice

With the availability of computer-scored tests and test banks provided by the book publishers, multiple-choice tests have become the most commonly used form of testing tool used in the U.S. today (in other parts of the world essay tests still dominate the evaluation arena). Developed correctly, multiple-choice questions are effective and can differentiate those students who know the subject from those who don't.

Pro:

- Easy to grade.

- Evaluates how well a student recognizes the right answer rather than how well a student can recall memorized information in detail (as they would have to do for an essay question). Easier for students who have trouble recalling facts and figures.

- Covers a lot of material in a short period of time.

- Questions often available from test banks developed by textbook publishers.

Con:

- Development can be a time-consuming process if you really want to develop valid and reliable questions.

- Some students are good at process-of-elimination thinking that multiple-choice tests favor, while others are not.

- Multiple-choice tests are good at testing recall of memorized facts and data, but are not as effective in testing analytical ability.

Developing multiple-choice questions

Distracters: As you are developing your multiple-choice exams, think about the incorrect answers you develop as "distracters." Good distracters will draw in students who have not studied the subject as thoroughly as they should have. Poorly developed distracters will draw in even those who have studied well. Develop questions that have at least four possible answers in order to minimize the guessing factor. The worst multiple-choice questions are trick questions that are of little value except to determine which students are good at answering trick questions.

Textbook test banks: People who have little formal training in building tests sometimes are asked by textbook authors to design test banks for their books. Make sure you carefully review each question you select from a test bank, and even then use with caution.

All of the above: Do not confuse students by using answers like "all of the above" or "none of the above." These are particularly difficult for international students because students have to weigh all answers in the universe of answers, and this in a language that is often not their native tongue.

Consistency: Use a consistent sentence format on every test (e.g., question length, what part of the questions and responses you capitalize, what punctuation you use, etc.).

Impossible answers: Do not include answers that are clearly impossible. These are easily eliminated by students and make guessing the right answer easier.

Using qualifiers: Do not use qualifiers like "always" or "usually." Each person has a different idea of how much or how little these terms cover.

Using negatives: Avoid using negatives such as "Which of the following is not the reason to accept the theory of relative co-analysis?" That just makes the question a mind game and twice as difficult to answer (particularly for international students).

Question and answer length: Most of the subject matter should be in the question itself. The correct answer and the distracters should be as short as possible.

 Choosing the Most Appropriate: **If you feel there might still be a question as to the choice of two answers that are very close in meaning, you might want to include in the question the note, "Choose the most appropriate answer."**

Grading multiple-choice tests

The simplest way to grade multiple-choice questions is to use a grading key. Take a blank test, mark it at the top with the word "KEY" and circle the correct answers. You should circle the correct answers in a color that is different than the one you are going to use to grade the actual tests. This will minimize the chance you will mix up the answer key and the students' tests. It works best if you circle the correct answer on the answer key with a felt tip marker and then use a regular ballpoint pen to grade the tests.

You can also make an answer sheet that you can overlay on multiple-choice questions by cutting out the area around the correct responses on an extra copy of your test. Using a hand punch with a large cutout area works well if the responses are close enough to the edge to get the punch over the correct answer choice (if you justify your questions and answers as far to the left of the page as possible, it will help). You can then quickly count the number of correct responses. You need to be careful when using this method that students have not marked more than one answer for each question.

For larger classes most schools provide machine-graded, multiple-choice answer forms that you can hand out with your tests. Check with your department head to determine if your school offers this option. Machine grading can make your job much easier when teaching large classes. The software available with these machine-grading systems can also help you in determining how effective and reliable your test questions are.

T
I
P

Stop Cheating Before It Starts: **Don't just put a checkmark by the correctly answered question and a cross (or nothing at all) by an incorrectly answered answer on a multiple-choice test. Students have been known to change an answer when teachers hand back a graded test for review by circling the correct answer and blocking out the incorrect one as if they had made a mistake while taking the test and had corrected it before turning it in. It's always best to cross through or circle the correct answer when a student answers a question incorrectly. The honest student will know which question he or she missed, and the dishonest student will not be able to cheat because he or she knows that when you graded the exam there was no mark on that particular answer.**

Multiple Choice and Machine Grading: **When using mechanical grading equipment to grade tests that are a mixture of multiple-choice and essay/fill-in questions, make sure you put all the multiple-choice questions first and the essay/fill-in last. Otherwise machine grading will be difficult due to the mixture of question types. If you happen to develop a mixed format exam by mistake, tell your class to answer all essay/fill-in questions as "A" on the multiple choice answer sheet and provide a written answer on the test form itself.**

Fill-in-the-Blank

Fill-in-the-blank questions test the recall of terms. In essence, it's a test of how well someone has memorized a word or phrase. If it's important enough that someone memorize a specific word or phrase, then test for it.

Pro:

- Easy to develop.

- Relatively easy to grade.

- Requires a specific answer rather than something that can be guessed from a choice of possible answers.

Con:

- Time consuming for students who can't remember the correct answer during the test and who waste a lot of test time trying.

- Particularly difficult for older students purely because of how age affects recall capabilities.

Other Testing Tools

Bonus questions

It's always a temptation for new teachers to add bonus questions to a test to give their students "a little extra chance." In fact, using bonus questions on every test is like curving; students come to believe that they can slack off a little because they know there will be a bonus question at the end of each exam to help lift their scores.

Bonus questions should only be used:

✓ To reward a class that has been working hard.

✓ To help a class that does not test well (e.g., where there is a large number of foreign students or nontraditional students who are in need of the extra help).

✓ To give you more flexibility. On a final exam you may decide not to assign points to a bonus question and tell your class that it will be up to your discretion how much you will add to the grade, by weighing the value of all the answers you receive before assigning a final value. This gives you the option of adding in the number of points you feel necessary to bring the overall scores up to a more realistic level, given the make-up of the class (a simple form of curving).

Impartial Extra Credit: **If you want to give extra credit outside of testing, have students summarize a relevant article. Remember though, if you give the opportunity to one you have to give it to the whole class to be totally impartial. And you have to take the time to grade it.**

Open-book tests

With open-book exams some students may feel compelled to look up an answer even if they don't have a clue to what the answer is or where to find it. They can waste an inordinate amount of time wading through pages of text trying to stumble across the answer. In some cases, students don't study at all and hope to be able to scrape through by looking up enough answers to get a passing grade. This does not work well for many courses. However, when you are teaching a class that requires higher order intellectual and problem-solving skills, open-book exams are useful. For example, teachers in the physical sciences may use an open-book test so that students don't have to memorize every formula, but can solve complex problems by applying the relevant formula in the book to the problem at hand.

Show Open-Book Examples: **If you plan to use open-book exams, provide your students with sample questions before your first test. These examples should make it clear that the questions will be harder than questions would be on a comparable closed book exam and emphasize that prior study and understanding of the material are a must.**

Take-home tests

Another shadowy area in the realm of student evaluation in higher education is the use of take-home tests. Students often get together to respond to take-home tests, so these kinds of tests quickly lose their evaluative power. You might want to use a take-home test if it covers some sort of case or problem analysis that:

✓ Students cannot complete in the time allotted for a test in the classroom.

✓ Requires complex thinking and analysis of a problem.

✓ Requires supplementary research.

When you really get down to it, a take-home test is just another form of class project.

Take-home Test Form: **If you give take-home tests, the top sheet of the test should be a sign-off sheet on which students confirm that they did not receive help from others to complete the assignment and that the work is completely their own. This form would have to be signed by each student before handing the test in for evaluation. Check to see if your school has an academic integrity honor system and use the same wording in your sign-off sheet.**

Quizzes

Quizzes, and particularly unannounced quizzes (also known as "pop" quizzes), are not the flavor-of-the-day for most students. In fact, many nontraditional students (particularly those taking night classes) feel unannounced quizzes should be used only with traditional, full-time students. Yet, if pop quizzes are structured correctly they can be a good indicator of whether students are keeping up with the material. If you feel quizzes are a necessary part of your teaching arsenal, use them, no matter the type of students you teach.

Daily Quizzes: **Some teachers put quiz questions in their syllabi that correspond to each chapter in the textbook. At the beginning of each class the teacher gives a quick, two- to three-minute quiz using a few of the quiz questions in the syllabus. This helps ensure that students are reading the material before class. Students often complain about this system throughout the term, and then thank the professor after the term is over because they were "motivated" to study before each class rather than waiting until exam time to cram all the material in.**

Why Give Quizzes? **Tell your students during the first class why you are using quizzes, that is, to evaluate how well they are keeping up with the material. This will help reduce the friction quizzes often generate.**

NOTES:

Chapter 13

Building and Administering Your Tests

In this chapter:

Tips for Building Tests

Skill levels

An exam should be written to an eighth- or ninth-grade reading level. This will help ensure that most of the students have the capacity to understand the words and structure of the test. Most tests should not be designed to test reading ability along with the actual subject matter the test is testing, unless reading ability is one of the subjects being tested.

To also make your test easier to read, you should:

✔ Always number the test questions. This will help with class discussions of the test questions.

✔ Make sure there is enough "white space" on the page to make the questions easy to read.

✔ Make sure you allow enough space on the page for students to respond to the question. If you allow students to write on the back of the page, make sure you indicate in the instructions how they are to use the back page.

Test length

Whenever you finish developing a test ask yourself if the average student in your class could finish the test in the time allotted. It can take two to three times longer for a student to take an exam than it takes the teacher who wrote the exam to take it. Some students will finish very quickly, and some will take right up until the last minute to complete the test. And it doesn't always follow that it's the best students who finish first. It's often a matter of both the student's learning capacity and style of responding to test questions. Some people answer a question and move on quickly to the next, never returning to that question while others answer a question and return later for further verification.

Correctly estimating how long it will take your students to complete a test is an art. Ask other teachers for their input. You will find that it depends on the type of questions you ask and the depth of analysis you require. As you become more experienced in developing and giving tests you will become more adept at estimating test taking time. Until you have a good feeling for how long it takes, record the actual time it takes students to complete your tests so you can use this information in estimating testing time the next time you design a test. You can do this by noting the time the first student turns in his or her test, what percentage of tests have been turned in by the mid-point and three-quarters of the way through the test, and the time the last student turns a test in.

Minimizing errors

Nothing is more embarrassing than having a student point out an error on a test. If you wait until the last minute to start putting your test together, errors often result. Begin early in the term to pull together the questions you plan to use in your exams. As you outline chapters and review your notes, copy down those topics you feel should be tested for and begin building the questions to test for them. Take your time reading and revising your questions to make sure they are as bulletproof as you can make them when they appear on the final draft of your test.

Let someone else read over your exam before making the final copies for your class. There is a tendency for teachers to overlook obvious problem areas because they are too close to the test development process. Letting an impartial third party look at the exam will ensure that the test is as logical and unbiased as possible.

Reviewing for tests

If time permits, it always helps to leave some time available during the last class before a test to review major points with students. This is to make sure that there are no outstanding questions and that students will know which points you consider most important (and therefore the ones they should spend the most time on when studying for the test).

Using test banks

Textbook authors often include test banks on computer disks that you can use to develop your own tests. As mentioned earlier, a good author is not necessarily a good test developer. Early test banks were pretty rough and in far too many cases developed by the author's teaching assistant. Today many authors, aware of the bad reputation of past test banks, are trying to clean up their act. You might want to call up the author and ask him or her who developed the questions, just to make sure of the level of developer whose product you are reviewing.

Voice

Students can often tell when a test bank is used to build an exam. The "voice" or language of the test questions is different than the voice of the lectures and discussions the teacher leads in class. Each teacher presents material in a different way because of educational background, past experiences, culture, etc. This means the words he or she uses in class presentations will often be different than those used by a book's author to develop test questions. If you use test banks to develop your tests (which most teachers do) and you want a test that is reliable and one that tests what it is supposed to test, you need to look at every question and ask yourself:

1. Is this the language I used when presenting the material in class?

2. Is this how I would have asked this question to obtain the response I want?

If you answer "no" to either of these questions, you need to review the language of the question and revise it to reflect your teaching style and objectives. Many teachers use the test bank questions that are included in the instructor's manual/resource guide to build their own question banks, rather than using the questions without any modification. This includes essay as well as multiple-choice questions.

Your own personal test bank

One of the handiest things you can do to make test development easier is to begin developing your own test questions early in the term. As soon as you begin reading the materials, jot down the ideas you feel are important or concepts you want students to be able to grasp from the materials presented. Put them in a separate notebook or computer file. At the same time you can begin designing questions to address the particular topics you feel are important and put them in the same notebook or file. This could include questions from a textbook test bank you have modified to reflect your own voice. Then when test time comes around, you will have a question bank to go to when building your test.

Question order

The more comfortable you can make students as they take a test, the more effective the test will be in evaluating a student's work. It's always best to start out with easy questions and then move to the more difficult ones.

Randomizing the choices

Many students, after answering four consecutive questions with the same letter option (e.g. B, B, B, B), may begin to think they have made a mistake somewhere because there are too many answers using the same letter. Some may even change their answers in response to this fear. To avoid the problem you can use a random order generator to allocate letter answers to questions. Many textbook publishers offer this option when building a test using their software. Another solution is to tell your students up front that you make the test up without considering the order of the correct answers. Let them know there could be a whole page of B's or D's. This will help alleviate the anxiety among the students and get you off the hook when you don't have the time to randomize the answer choices.

Problems with question strings

Another question order problem that some teachers run into is developing a test question whose answer depends on the answer in a previous question. This can be a very tricky way to develop a test question, a question that can also be very time-consuming to grade. If the student gets the first question wrong, but the logic in the second question is correct, are you going to penalize the student for getting the second question wrong just because he or she missed the first one? If you want to use these types of questions, it will mean following the logic from question to question to make sure you fairly grade the students' analytical ability, even though one of the answers may be incorrect. This type of question is most commonly used in mathematics and in the physical sciences.

Giving directions

On the day of the test your students' attention will be focussed on the information they have crammed into their heads while studying for your test. Therefore, only part of their attention will be on any verbal directions you give before the test begins. That's why it's important to print clear and detailed instructions on the test about what is expected so the students can refer back to it during the test period without having to ask you for clarification.

You should also clearly indicate on the test how many points each question is worth. This will help students prioritize the questions as they work through the test. One exception to this rule concerns bonus or extra credit questions. As mentioned earlier, you may assign points, but some teachers prefer to wait until they have had a chance to review responses before assigning points. This gives the teacher the flexibility of deciding the number of points to apply depending on the quality of the students' overall responses to a particular bonus question.

Deciding on question type

For each subject topic you need to decide if you want to ask a question that requires the student to simply recall memorized information or to provide a more detailed analysis of information for which some original thinking is required. Both types of questions have value depending on the type of material being tested. Questions that ask for more original thinking will take extra time to develop, so make sure you allow for the extra time in your development process. You may want to use "dual-task" questions in which you ask a question with a two-part answer. The first part asks the student to recall memorized information. The second part asks the student to use the memorized information to give a more in-depth analysis and solution to a problem.

Questions That Match Your Style: **Make sure the type of questions you ask match your teaching style. For example, if you spend your time in class focusing on developing your students' critical thinking skills and your tests ask for simple recall of facts and figures, there is a major disconnect there for students taking the tests.**

Making up answer keys

Make up an answer key to your test <u>before</u> you give the test. You'll be surprised how this helps you catch any last-minute errors. It also alerts you to any response patterns that appear in your test (e.g., multiple-choice answers) that a test-savvy student might be able to use to his or her advantage. You should also write out the responses that you want to see in essay questions. By doing this ahead of time, you can validate whether the question elicits the response you expect.

A Test Building Checklist

Use the following checklist after the first draft of your test is completed to see if you have covered all the bases:

✓ Make sure your test question numbers are sequential and that incorporating questions from a test bank or your own past tests has not changed the number order.

✓ Make sure that for multiple-choice questions your choices are lettered sequentially (A, B, C, D, etc.). Sometimes word processing software can cause problems in sequential lettering, particular the last choice (e.g. changing a D to an E when you hit enter after typing the last choice).

✓ Make sure that there is enough space for the students to answer essay and fill-in-the-blank questions.

✓ Make sure you don't have duplicate questions on the same test. One way of doing this is to take a draft copy and write a word or two in the left margin that explains the topic of the question. You can then review your margin notes to see what questions address what subject.

✓ Make sure your questions add up to the score you expect them to. For example, if you have a test consisting of 30 multiple-choice questions and 5 essay questions, and you want them to add up to 100, you could give each multiple-choice question a value of two points and each essay a value of eight points. This is in contrast to the 50-point total you would have if you multiplied the multiple-choice questions by one each and the essays by four each.

✓ Make sure the date on the top of your test is the actual test date, not the date of the night you were developing the test or the date from a previous term's exam you were using as a template.

✓ Make sure each answer can be found in either the textbook (this term's book, not last term's book), your lecture notes, or other materials you have had the students review.

✓ Make sure the answer choices on multiple-choice questions have enough information in them and are well defined enough to clearly indicate the correct answer choice to the student who knows the correct answer.

✓ Complete your answer key before you give the exam.

Reading Twice Is Once Too Long: **If in reading over the questions you have to read a question twice before answering it, eliminate that question (or reword it to make it simpler to understand on the first read-through). A question that has to be read twice before being understood is a time waster.**

Administering Tests

Handing out tests

Students should have the maximum amount of time to take the test. If your class is large, this means you need to minimize the time it takes to pass out the test. You don't want the people in the back of the room penalized because they receive their exams last. If possible, have a colleague help pass out tests. Or split up the pile and send half the tests down each side of the room.

Two Tests Are Too Many: **It can be incredibly time consuming to grade two or more sets of questions. It is better to convince your students early on that you are going to be on the lookout for cheating rather than to double your workload by handing out two different tests.**

Dealing with your mistakes

No matter how hard you try, there will come a time when you develop a test in which a word has been misspelled, a question poorly phrased, a key word transposed, etc. That's life. Therefore, be open to students who come up to you with what they think is a problem with one of your questions. If you do find a problem with a question after the test has begun, you can either put it on the board or announce it to the class. It's your call. Just be aware that announcing things during a test can be very disruptive to a student's concentration. Yet, if the error is a major one, announce it.

Discussing Problems: **When discussing possible test flaws with students, make sure you do it up at your desk. Don't disturb other students by discussing it at the student's seat.**

Minimizing test stress

✓ Let your students know in advance how you structure your tests and why. If there is time, give them a copy of a prototype test so they can become familiar with your testing style.

✓ Always arrive on the day of the test on time or if at all possible, early. Coming into the classroom out of breath just before you give a test does not help reduce student stress. If you are calm and collected, your students will appreciate this lower level of anxiety. And smile!

✓ Pitch your voice low and give test directions in a clear and calm voice.

✓ Carry extra supplies with you (calculators, pencils, pens, etc.) that students can borrow if they have forgotten theirs in the rush to get to class.

Dealing with cheating

Whether we like it or not cheating happens, and it probably happens more than we would like to believe it does. Let your students know from the very start that you will not tolerate cheating of any kind. Some teachers ask students to take different seats the day of a test to ensure there is no cheating among neighbors. Other teachers develop more than one version of the same test.

A few ways to help students avoid the temptation to cheat is:

✓ Ensure that all notes and books are under a student's desk when the test begins.

✓ Although it is common to want to read something while students are taking a test, you should either avoid reading altogether and keep an eye on the class or when reading, make it a habit to look up every five minutes or so and survey the class. This is to just to let the students know you are keeping an eye on their progress.

✓ Don't let your students keep your tests after they are graded. Hand them back to the students after grading, discuss them, and have the students turn them back in. Tests have a tendency to circulate quickly around campus once handed back. If you do allow your students to keep your tests it puts the burden on you to come up with different questions for each new test of the same material.

 Using Study Guides: **One alternative to allowing your students to keep their old tests to review for a final exam is to hand out a study guide before the final exam that outlines the topics you feel are most important.**

Tips on Grading Tests

One page at a time

If you are grading a multiple-choice test by hand, grade the first page of the test for each student and turn the page. Then the second page and turn the page, then the third page and turn the page, and so on. For example, if you have 20 tests, grade page one of all 20 tests before moving on to page two. Grading objective questions in this manner helps you develop a tempo. When grading essays, grade each student's response to a specific question and then move on to the next question. This will help you maintain consistency across responses.

With longer essay questions it's best to read all (or at least as many as possible) of the essays first to get an idea as to the average level of understanding. Then go back, and using the grading method illustrated earlier, grade each essay.

✓ Use an ink color other than red to grade tests. Red means bad news. And a page full of red ink is not the best reinforcement for the student to try to do better on the next test.

✓ If you want to be as fair as possible when grading essay tests, have the students put their names on the back of the tests rather than on the front. Or, begin grading the last page first and work forward so that the last page you grade is the cover page with the name at the top. In this way you won't know whose handwriting belongs to which student until you have finished grading the test.

Handwriting Bias: **There are some students who are just more organized than others. There are some that have better handwriting than others. In neither case should a student get preferential treatment because of it. If you clearly lay out your grading criteria ahead of time, you will be less likely to be swayed by good handwriting alone.**

What to do with poor questions

If you see that an excessive number of students have answered a question incorrectly, list the question number on a pad of paper and tick off the number of students that selected each answer choice (e.g., A, B, C, D, etc.). If one distracter option pulled more than half the students, or pulled more than the correct answer, go back to your notes and make sure you covered the point(s) adequately in class. Review the original question to see if it was correctly worded. If you find there could have been misunderstanding, then throw the question out.

The Value of Machine Grading: **If you use a mechanical grading system (e.g., Scantron®) to grade multiple-choice questions, learn how to use the validation software that often comes with it. The software can give you a detailed analysis of how well your questions and answers worked in testing for the knowledge you were looking for.**

Take your time

Don't try to grade the whole test in one setting. Two hours is probably the most you'll want to spend grading a test without taking a break.

Better Answers Than Your Own: **As was mentioned earlier, you may find students who actually come up with an answer that's better than your own. Be open to making changes on your grading key.**

Timely Grading Is Key: **Even though it's important to pace yourself when grading tests, don't let too much time elapse between the time you grade the test and when you return it for discussion. If you wait too long students will have moved on mentally to the next subject and you will have lost an excellent opportunity to reinforce material already learned.**

Use a Grading System: **Try to grade each set of tests the same way. Once you have a system that works well, stay with it. This will ensure reliability across the grading tasks.**

Listen to the Wrong Answers, Too: **You can learn a lot about your class' understanding of a particular topic by listening to students' wrong answers as well as their right answers. Wrong answers are good indicators of where you still need to do some work.**

Correcting for invalid test questions

If you find that a majority of your students consistently answered the same question incorrectly, and that a majority of the students who are answering the question incorrectly are the ones doing well on the rest of the test, then it's time to consider throwing out the question. If discarding the question throws off your grading points system you can use a little creative math to revise your system.

Suppose your original test was made up of 50 questions that were going to be worth two points each to add up to a total of 100 points. Then you found that you had to discard one question. Here is what you would do to adjust for the loss of one question:

Original number of test questions:	**50**
Number of questions discarded:	<u>**-1**</u>
Total number of valid questions:	**49**
Valid number of questions divided by original number of questions:	**49/50 = .98**

Let's suppose a student's score on this test was 46 after the elimination of the discarded question. That student's actual score on a 100 point scale would be 94. The calculation is 46 (new score) divided by .98 (valid question ratio) x 2 (value of each test question).

International students and testing

International students who come to the United States for schooling have to accept the fact that they cannot expect any favoritism over their American-born colleagues. For international students whose native language is not English, and who are having a hard time even though they are working very hard to keep up, you may decide that you want to build into the student's final score a small "language factor" to compensate for the lack of English skills. This is up to you. You have to know the student's level of English comprehension before making this decision. And, you have to be sure it's the language and not subject content that is holding back the student.

T I P

Responding to International Student Needs: **If you have a number of foreign students whose native language is not English, you may want to announce that if any foreign student has a question about the meaning of a certain word, and you can respond to the question without giving away the answer to a test question, you will do so.**

A L E R T

Dictionary Use: **Some foreign students will ask if they can use dictionaries during a test. Whether to let them or not will depend on the subject being taught and the type of dictionary used. Many foreign language dictionaries only give synonyms for English words. That is, they give a word for word translation. Others give full definitions. If there is a chance that the students can discern the answers to test questions from looking through a foreign language dictionary, then you should not permit it. It will give an unfair advantage to the foreign students. If, on the other hand, you do not believe they can discern answers by using a dictionary (e.g., when using a synonym-only dictionary), you should consider letting them use it. Ask to see the student's dictionary before you allow its use.**

The Perfect Test?

There is no such thing as the perfect test. Each teacher develops the kind of test he or she feels best evaluates the subject being taught and the way it is taught. As you develop more tests the job will get easier. Many teachers find a mixture of the above tools (multiple-choice, essay, fill-in-the-blank) is the best way to test the full breadth of a student's knowledge. What mixture you use will depend on several things:

✓ The time you have available to develop the test.

✓ The time you have available to give the test.

✓ The time you have available to grade the test.

You need to accept the fact that your first few tests may not be very good. Like everything else in teaching, it's a learning process. But, rest assured, you will become more proficient at developing and giving effective tests the more you do it.

NOTES:

Chapter 14

Other Evaluation Tools

In this chapter:

Assigning and Grading Homework

Homework is a quick check of a student's ability to understand a particular section of the course material at a particular point during the term. This is different from term papers, which are a cumulative analysis of all or a major part of the course material over the term period.

Whether you assign homework or not will depend on:

✓ Whether it will add significantly to the understanding of the class material.

✓ Whether you have time to grade it.

✓ Whether you have time to discuss it in class (if you feel this is important).

✓ Whether you think students have the time and/or basic knowledge level to complete the assignment(s).

Outside writing assignments are particularly important in classes where writing skills are emphasized (creative writing, business writing, American literature classics, great French philosophers, etc.). In these classes the learning takes place through the analysis and writing process. The length of the writing skills assignments will again greatly depend on the time you have to grade them.

Grading a writing assignment

The rules for grading a writing assignment are very similar to those for grading essay questions on a test. If there is time, you should read all the writing assignments through first without assigning a grade (or as many as you can). This will give you a feeling for the general quality level of the responses. Then, the second time through you should check off the points you feel have been covered by the student. To make the grading task easier many teachers write down beforehand the points they want to see made by each student. As the teacher reviews the assignment, he or she checks off the points as they are mentioned and adds the checkmarks to come up with a final grade.

There are several ways you can quickly evaluate a writing assignment:

A. Give a student an A for acceptable or U for unacceptable.

B. Grade using a point system (1-5, 1-100, etc.)

C. Use a check system similar to the one below:

✓++	=	95
✓+	=	85
✓	=	75
✓-	=	65
U (or X)	=	Unacceptable

***Grammar and International Students:* You may want to ask an international student whose native language is not English to let you review a draft of an assignment before turning it in. Then, if you find they need help with the grammar or sentence structure, advise them to find an English-speaking friend who can help them clean up the grammar for the final draft.**

Assigning and Grading Term Papers

Some teachers assign papers to see if students can write them. Others assign papers to see if students can apply concepts learned in the classroom to real-world situations. By applying concepts students show that they are able to assimilate information, understand it, and provide proof of this in a clear, concise, written presentation. To ensure that the process is a positive learning experience for the student, a teacher needs to be clear in his or her own mind about the purpose of the paper.

The process

When assigning papers you should advise and monitor a student's progress on:

✓ Choosing a topic.

✓ Finding valid information resources and reference materials.

✓ Developing a general structure for the paper.

If time allows, you might also want to review the first draft to make sure the student is heading in the right direction.

Instructions

Instructions should include how you want the final report to look (and why!) as well as how long it should be. If you require a bibliography, you should indicate how you want the bibliographic data presented.

Evaluation

Below are some of the criteria you can use to evaluate a student paper:

✓ Did the student seem to understand the subject matter?

✓ Was the topic presented in the paper relevant to the subject matter discussed in class?

✓ Did the student cover the topic adequately?

✓ How well was the information organized?

✓ How well was data presented? Was it clear or ambiguous?

✓ How accurate was the information presented?

✓ How logical was the paper's structure?

- Main theme
- Analysis of information
- Conclusion(s)

✓ Did the paper flow well or was it scattered or broken in spots?

✔ How original was the paper?

✔ Did the student turn the paper in on time?

✔ Did the student follow your instructions?

✔ Is the paper in the specified format?

✔ Did the student use correct grammar and syntax?

✔ Did the student's writing style add to or detract from the effectiveness of the paper?

✔ How extensive was the bibliography?

✔ Did the student use the correct form when citing references?

✔ Did the student adequately proofread the paper?

Grading term papers

The same method can be used in grading papers as is used in grading any written material. See "Grading a writing assignment" earlier in the chapter.

Assigning and Grading Group Projects

When assigning a paper there is usually only one student involved, while for a project there is often more than one student responsible for the final report. You may also require a final presentation for a group project. The major difference between a paper and a group project is you are evaluating not only the final outcome (a paper, a presentation, etc.), but the teamwork that is a result of a group of students working together to come to a unified conclusion (hopefully).

There are two primary methods of grading group projects. In one, students rate each other's efforts before the final project grade is known. This is called pre-grade weighting. In the other method, called post-grade weighting, the teacher assigns a team grade for the project and the team members determine what part of that grade should be allocated to each team member. NOTE: In both cases it is the teacher who determines the final grade. Following are examples of each method.

Pre-grade weighting

Using the pre-grade weighting system, students are not given their individual project scores until the individual ratings have been turned in to the teacher. The total project score will be adjusted by the teacher using the sum of the individual performance ratings each team member receives from his or her colleagues. The individual project scores will then be given to each student by the teacher.

The scoring process is as follows:

✓ Each student is to confidentially rate each team member (including him or herself) by dividing up 100 points among the team members.

✓ Students should be told that as a result of the team rating, an individual student's final grade will not be more than 15 percent above or 15 percent below the total project score given by the teacher.

✓ All scores must be whole numbers.

✓ The final project score cannot exceed 100 for each student.

Let's look at how this scoring method would be used to rate a team of four students:

Project Rating Scores				
	John	Pam	Justin	Mary
John's scoring of:	30 pts	25 pts	15 pts	30 pts
Pam's scoring of:	40 pts	25 pts	15 pts	20 pts
Justin's scoring of:	30 pts	25 pts	20 pts	25 pts
Mary's scoring of:	40 pts	25 pts	10 pts	25 pts
Average score	140 pts	100 pts	60 pts	100 pts

From the scoring you can see that John did a significant amount of the work on the project (140 points). The person who probably did not carry his part of the workload was Justin (60 points). Both of the other teammates worked at a level that was required to complete the project satisfactorily. If the overall project grade given by the teacher was 87 points out of 100, then using the pre-grade weighting calculation, John could receive as much as 122 points (1.40 * 87 = 122). Since 100 is the highest grade possible, John's final grade would be 100, not 122. By doing the arithmetic Justin earned an individual grade of 52 (.60 * 87). Yet, because of the grading limits built into the scoring process, that no score can be more than 15 percent higher (87 + 15% = 100) or 15 percent lower (87 - 15% = 74) than the total project grade, Justin would receive a final grade of 74, not 52. Both Pam and Mary would receive a grade of 87 because their performance scores were both 100 points (1.00 * 87).

Post-grade weighting

In this case the teacher grades the project first. The teacher then gives the group team members a total project grade and asks each student to rate their teammate's performance using this grade as a basis. The students then distribute the total available actual scores among the team members. In the above example the team members would have 4 * 87 or 348 points to distribute among themselves.

The scoring process is as follows:

✓ Each student is to confidentially rate each team member (including him or herself) using the total project score multiplied by the number of team members as the total available number of rating points available.

✓ No individual team member can receive a rating higher than 100 from another team member.

✓ Students are to be told that no one can receive a final project grade that is 15 percent above the group project grade. Using the previous example, that would be 87 * 1.15 or 100 points.

✓ No one can receive a grade that is less than 50 percent of the group project grade. Using the previous example, this would be 87 * .50 or 44 points.

✓ All scores must be whole numbers.

Using the example given earlier, let's look at scores that result from using the post-grade weighting method:

Project Rating Scores				
	John	Pam	Justin	Mary
John's scoring of:	100 pts	87 pts	70 pts	91 pts
Pam's scoring of:	100 pts	90 pts	71 pts	87 pts
Justin's scoring of:	100 pts	81 pts	80 pts	87 pts
Mary's scoring of:	<u>100 pts</u>	<u>87 pts</u>	<u>74 pts</u>	<u>87 pts</u>
Average score	100 pts	86 pts	74 pts	88 pts

Using the post-grade weighting method, John's average performance score is 100 and therefore he would receive a final grade of 100. Justin only received 74 performance points and therefore would receive that amount as his final grade. Mary would receive a final grade of 88 and Pam an 86. The total of the average scores (100 + 86 + 74 + 88) is the 348 points assigned by the teacher.

Students are often more serious about the team member evaluation process using the post-grade weighting method because they know exactly what is at stake. Even though they know the teacher has the final say, they have to deal with a fixed number of points that are to be divided up among the team members. When using the pre-grade weighting method the team does not know what the total team score is before rating their colleagues' performance, and therefore their perception of the impact on their grades is not as acute. Actual use of the two methods will tell you which best fits your own evaluation style.

**Confidentiality Is Key:** Using either method, it is important that the individual team member scoring be done confidentially so that each team member does not know the score given by the other members.

Project rating criteria

When students are required to rate other students, you need to give them a list of behavioral criteria upon which to base their individual rating choices. A sample team evaluation form is shown on the next page.

The student team members need to be told that instead of rating their fellow students on subjective points (for example, Mary has a great personality), they should use an evaluation form based on the criteria below to analyze their classmates' performance. They might rate performance on a scale of 1 to 5 (for example, Mary attended every team meeting and therefore deserves a rating of 5 on meeting attendance). After adding up all the category scores, each team member should have a firmer basis on which to rate their teammates' performance.

Team Evaluation Form

Instructions: You are to complete one of these forms for each member of your team. Your ratings are confidential and will be added to the ratings of the other team members to come up with a total score for each team member.

Team member being evaluated: _____

Task	Poor				Good
Attendance at team meetings.	1	2	3	4	5
Quality of contributions to team discussions.	1	2	3	4	5
Quality of performance on team assignments.	1	2	3	4	5
Cooperation with other team members.	1	2	3	4	5
Contribution of new or innovative ideas.	1	2	3	4	5
On time completion of tasks.	1	2	3	4	5
Ability to work well under stress.	1	2	3	4	5
Willingness to practice for oral presentations.	1	2	3	4	5
TOTAL SCORE (out of 40)					

Unfortunately, you will often find students sticking together and agreeing beforehand on the percentages they will be giving each other because they don't want to hurt fellow students by giving them low scores. Therefore, these rating methods are best used to give the teacher an overall view of who really worked hard and who really didn't do much at all.

 Relating to Workplace: **Make sure to emphasize with students that the teamwork required in a project is good practice for future project assignments in the workplace.**

Project presentations

Although a project can end with a submitted paper, many teachers have groups present their projects to the whole class at the end of the term. To ensure that presentations are effective learning tools you have to decide early on what the major objective of the project is to be. Your objectives might be:

✓ To have the students do the research work, provide a document, and make a presentation that shows they have learned something about the application of the subject matter to the outside world.

✓ To have students demonstrate the skills needed to make effective presentations.

✓ To demonstrate that group members can work effectively as a team.

The points above demand three different skill sets. Make sure you decide which skills you are most interested in before the project is assigned, and let your students know when you assign the project work which ones you will be grading most heavily on.

If you want your students to do group presentations, there are several things you should consider. One is the reason for the presentation in the first place. It should be for the benefit of the rest of the class, as well as the students who are giving the presentation. In fact, the key to determining if a project presentation was successful is to find out if the student audience understood the major points presented.

Using Team Strengths: **An example of using team strengths to accomplish a team goal would be where a team might decide who are the best presenters on the team and have only those people do the actual presenting.**

They Are Not Professionals: **Students, particularly traditional students just out of high school, are not usually adept at making crisp, clean, professional presentations. They often have had no experience in making effective presentations and those who do present well often have personalities that lend themselves to making presentations in front of groups. If content, research, and problem analysis are the most important elements of the process for you, the actual presentation of the project results should receive the least amount of weight in the grading process. You might also want to consider curving the presentation grade to be fair to those whose presentation skills are not as good, but whose work on the analytical and research side of the project was good. Some teachers base 85 percent to 90 percent of the project grade on content and 10 percent to 15 percent on the quality of a final presentation.**

The Final Evaluation: **In evaluating a project, remember that it's the final paper that shows the real work that was done and what was learned in the process of completing the project.**

Don't Waste Time on Too Much Commentary: **If it's the end of the term, don't waste time writing reams of commentary on projects that you are going to be handing back the last day of class. Most students are only going to give it a cursory look because it's the end of the term. In this situation it's best to give a general synopsis of your feelings about the paper, enough to give them a general idea of how well they did and why. If you like, you can let students know that if they would like a more detailed analysis they should contact you at the beginning of the next term.**

Grading Cases

Cases are graded much like an essay test would be graded, with some important differences. Remember when we said earlier that a key to analyzing a case successfully is to identify its real problem. Yet, even if students do not identify the most critical problem confronting the object of the case, they may still have done an excellent analysis of what they thought the real problem was. This means you will have to follow the reasoning of each student, whether or not it refers to the real problem. This makes grading cases somewhat more complex than grading essay questions on a test where a particular answer may be the only acceptable answer. You will have to evaluate how well students develop alternative solutions to a problem and then on what basis they select what they feel is the most effective solution. In essence, it's like grading an essay question with several parts. You will have to evaluate each part separately and score each as a separate part of the complete case analysis problem.

You might use a case evaluation form like the one that follows to grade your students' cases. There are 20 criteria worth a maximum of 5 points apiece for a total of 100 possible points.

CASE EVALUATION FORM

Criteria	Rating
Organization and Presentation	
✓ Organization of report was easy to follow	1 2 3 4 5
✓ Correct spelling and grammar used	1 2 3 4 5
✓ Writing style was interesting and effective in getting points across	1 2 3 4 5
✓ Balance maintained between problem definition, analysis, solution(s), and recommendation(s)	1 2 3 4 5

Case Evaluation Form (cont'd)

Content					
A. Problem definition					
✔ Case problem(s) correctly identified	1	2	3	4	5
✔ Statement of problem(s) was clear and concise	1	2	3	4	5
✔ Both immediate and long-range problems were considered	1	2	3	4	5
B. Analysis of causes					
✔ Distinguished between symptoms and causes	1	2	3	4	5
✔ Distinguished between fact, and student's own assumptions	1	2	3	4	5
✔ Recognized all important factors surrounding causes	1	2	3	4	5
✔ Avoided excessive restating of case facts	1	2	3	4	5
✔ Analysis reflected solid understanding of relevant course concepts	1	2	3	4	5
C. Solutions					
✔ All practical solutions identified	1	2	3	4	5
✔ Solutions consistent with definition of problem(s)	1	2	3	4	5
✔ Each solution evaluated in terms of feasibility	1	2	3	4	5
✔ Recommended solution clearly stated	1	2	3	4	5
✔ The solution followed logically from the analysis	1	2	3	4	5
✔ Implementation of solution was discussed	1	2	3	4	5

Case Evaluation Form (cont'd)

Research Conducted	
✔ Adequate for case	**1 2 3 4 5**
✔ Appropriate for case issues	**1 2 3 4 5**
TOTAL POINTS	**_____/ 100**
Comments:	

**Casework Analysis:** Teachers should emphasize when introducing casework that students have "particular knowledge" (from textbook and lectures) that will help them understand the case and be able to analyze it effectively. This information is found in class presentations, textbooks, and outside reading, if required.

Grading Attendance

Good or poor attendance should affect the class participation grade in a positive or negative way. It should be emphasized during the first class that attendance is important because of the extra material that is presented and discussed during class. Full-time students should almost always be evaluated on attendance. Part-time students should probably not be evaluated as heavily on attendance because they can have justifiable job conflicts that can affect their attendance record. Yet, you should still record part-time student attendance because it may be important for you to know if a student was in class when you were covering a particular subject. That student may complain later that you had not covered a particular subject on a test when in fact your records show he or she was absent at the time you covered the subject in question.

You need to clearly indicate in the syllabus your attendance policy and then keep good records. Some teachers use the "three classes missed" rule: If students miss more than three classes they lose a certain percentage of their point grade. Or their final grade is reduced by a half or whole grade, depending on the grading system used.

Attendance Policies: Some schools have attendance policies that must be followed. Check with your supervisor.

Grading Class Participation

How Much Weight Do You Give It?

The amount of class participation and the quality of class participation that you can expect is directly related to:

✓ The number of students in the class

✓ The time of day that the class is held

✓ The subject that is being taught

✓ The type of student (for example, traditional vs. nontraditional)

✓ Each student's motivation for being in your class.

Part-time teachers often encourage class participation as a part of their teaching style. You will need to know how best to motivate students to participate depending on the variables listed above. Even if the variables are the same from term to term, the amount and quality of class participation can still vary greatly between classes.

It's important to understand from the outset that there will always be someone in your class who is just too shy or too disinterested to participate in the class discussions. If you have made the effort to get these students involved in the class discussion and have had little or no success, you will have to refocus your attention on those in your class who are willing to participate. It might be a cynical way to look at it, but this is where the maximum pay-off is for all your students and the best use of your skills and time.

What Is "Quality" Class Participation?

Give your students an idea of what you mean by "quality" participation from the very start. For example, quality participation could mean:

✓ Regular attendance

✓ Adding insight to a discussion

✓ Providing interesting ideas

✓ Giving real-life/practical examples to illustrate points

✓ Responding to questions asked in class

✓ Participating actively in class discussions

There should be no participation points given if students just agree with what you have said.

***Quality, Not Quantity Participation:* Just because one student responds frequently does not mean that this student is contributing positively to the discussion. The student may be doing it just to get your attention. Listen for quality responses, not just paraphrasing of previously discussed facts or data.**

Some teachers use a checkmark system to record class participation efforts by students. During the discussion periods they keep the roster in front of them, and if a student responds in a quality way, the teacher puts a checkmark by that student's name. If the answer was particularly good the teacher might put two checkmarks by the student's name. This accomplishes two things. One, at the end of the term the teacher has a record of class participation for each student that he or she can use in the final grading process (by adding up all the checkmarks). And two, students can see how important the teacher considers the process because the teacher is evaluating their performance by making notations as they respond.

Participation Grade – Feedback: **Most students do not have a good feeling for how well they are or are not participating in a class. Giving students a mid-term class participation grade gives them feedback on how well they are doing and gives the student who wants to improve time to improve before the term ends. A good place to provide this update is on the last page of the mid-term exam when you are ready to hand it back after grading.**

Attendance As Part of Participation Grade: **If you are concerned about attendance, make sure you indicate what the consequences are of missing class in the syllabus. For example, you might say that three absences will reduce a student's grade by one grade level, or by a certain number of points.**

NOTES:

_____

_____

_____

_____

_____

_____

_____

_____

_____

_____

_____

_____

_____

Part V

You're Not Alone

APPENDIX

Where to Get Help!

In the following pages we've listed a number of references you can turn to when you run into problems not covered in this manual. Please be aware that we are not making recommendations as to the validity or reliability of any of the resources listed. You will need to do your own research to determine whether a particular organization or Web reference meets your needs. In addition, we have tried to include as many references as we possible, but we surely overlooked a few. When our Web site is completed at www.teachingbridge.com, we will include additional references as they become available.

We have tried to pull together the most current information available. That said, Web site and email addresses change almost on a daily basis. Should any of the information in the following lists change, these references should still contain enough contact data to help you find the information you need.

We have organized the appendix subjects as follows:

- **Associations and Professional Organizations** – organizations of teachers and other professionals that can provide you with the information you need to become a more effective teacher.

- **Reference Books/Bibliography** – books that were used to help write this manual as well as other books that provide additional information on teaching-related subjects.

- **Magazines, Newsletters, and Journals** – periodicals focussing on higher education.

- **International Resources** – a limited listing of higher education resources outside of the United States.

- **Textbook Publishers** – a selected list of the major textbook publishers serving schools in the United States.

- **Teaching Centers** – Over the last decade colleges and universities have been establishing teaching centers to enhance the skills of their teaching faculty. Many of these centers are on the Web. Our list is a place to start (many of the sites have links to other teaching center sites).

- **Internet Links in Higher Education** – These are links to Web pages that can provide assistance in any number of areas. Many of these sites focus on instructional technology and distance education.

- **Other Resources** – This section is a short list of resources not covered above.

Associations and Professional Organizations

Academy for Community College
  Leadership Advancement, Innovation
  & Modeling (ACCLAIM), Department of
  Adult and Community College Ed
NC State University
Campus Box 7801
Raleigh, NC 27695
Phone: (919) 515-6296
Fax: (919) 515-6305
Email: acclaim@ncsu.edu
Web: www2.ncsu.edu/ncsu/cep/acce/
  acclaim/acclaim.html

American Association for Adult and
  Continuing Education (AAACE)
1200 19th St., N.W., Suite 300
Washington, DC 20036
Phone: (202) 429-5131
Fax: (202) 223-4579
Web: www.albany.edu/aaace

American Association for Higher
  Education (AAHE)
One Dupont Circle, Suite 360
Washington, DC 20036
Phone: (202) 293-6440
Fax: (202) 293-0073
Email: info@aahe.org
Web: www.aahe.org

American Association for Vocational
  Instructional Materials
220 Smithonia Road
Winterville, GA 30683
Phone: (706) 742-5355
Fax: (706) 742-7005
Web: www.aavim.com

American Association of Colleges for
  Teacher Education
1307 New York Ave., N.W., Suite 300
Washington, DC 20005
Phone: (202) 293-2450
Fax: (202) 457-8095
Web: www.aacte.org

American Association of Community
  Colleges (AACC)
One Dupont Circle, N.W., Suite 410
Washington, DC 20036
Phone: (202) 728-0200
Fax: (202) 833-2467
Web: www.aacc.nche.edu

American Association of State Colleges
  and Universities (AASCU)
1307 New York Ave., N.W.,
Suite 700
Washington, DC 20005
Phone: (202) 293-7070
Fax: (202) 296-5819
Web: www.aascu.org

American Association of University
  Professors (AAUP)
1012 Fourteenth St., N.W., Suite 500
Washington, DC 20005
Phone: (800) 424-2973
Fax: (202) 737-5526
Email: aaup@aaup.org
Web: www.aaup.org

American Association of University
  Women (AAUW)
1111 16th St., NW
Washington, DC 20036
Phone: (800) 326-2289
Fax: (202) 872-1425
Email: info@mail.aauw.org
Web: www.aauw.org/home.html

American College Personnel
  Association (ACPA)
One Dupont Circle, N.W., Suite 300
Washington, DC 20036
Phone: (202) 835-2272
Fax: (202) 296-3286
Email: cgn@acpa.nche.edu
Web: www.acpa.nche.edu

American College Testing Inc.
2201 N. Dodge St.
Iowa City, IA 52243
Phone: (319) 337-1028
Fax: (319) 339-1059
Web: www.act.org

American Council on Education (ACE)
One Dupont Circle, N.W., Suite 800
Washington, DC 20036
Phone: (202) 939-9310
Fax: (202) 659-2212
Email: web@ace.nche.edu
Web: www.acenet.edu

American Educational Research
Association (AERA)
1230 Seventeenth St., N.W.
Washington, DC 20036
Phone: (202) 223-9485
Fax: (202) 775-1824
Email: wrussell@aera.net
Web: www.aera.net

American Evaluation Association (AEA)
P.O. Box 704
Point Reyes, CA 94956
Phone: (888) 311-6321
Fax: (415) 663-9601
Email: amevalassn@aol.com
Web: www.eval.org

Association for Career and Technical
Education (ACTE)
1410 King St.
Alexandria, VA 22314
Phone: (800) 826-9972
Fax: (703) 683-7424
Email: acte@acteonline.org
Web: www.avaonline.org

Association for Continuing Higher
Education (ACHE)
Trident Technical Community College
P.O. Box 118067, CE-M
Charleston, SC 29423
Phone: (803) 574-6658
Fax: (803) 574-6470
Email: zpwhelanwa@a.1.trident.tec.
sc.us
Web: www.charleston.net/org/ache/

Association for Educational
Communications and Technology
(AECT)
1025 Vermont Ave., N.W., Suite 820
Washington, DC 20005
Phone: (202) 347-7834
Fax: (202) 347-7839
Web: www.aect.org

Association of American Colleges and
Universities (AAC&U)
1818 R St., N.W.
Washington, DC 20009
Phone: (202) 387-3760
Fax: (202) 265-9532
Web: www.aacu-edu.org

Association of American Universities
(AAU)
1200 New York Ave., N.W., Suite 550
Washington, DC 20005
Phone: (202) 408-7500
Fax: (202) 408-8184
Web: www.tulane.edu/~aau

Association of College and Research
Libraries
American Library Association
50 E. Huron St.
Chicago, IL 60611
Phone: (800) 545-2433
Fax: (312) 280-2520
Email: acrl@ala.org
Web: www.ala.org/acrl.html

Association of Governing Boards of
Universities and Colleges
One Dupont Circle, Suite 400
Washington, DC 20036
Phone: (202) 296-8400
Fax: (202) 223-7053
Web: www.agb.org

Association of Teacher Educators
1900 Association Drive, Suite ATE
Reston, VA 20191
Phone: (703) 620-3110
Fax: (703) 620-9530
Email: ate1@aol.com
Web: www.siu.edu/departments/coe/ate

Career College Association (CCA)
10 G St., N.E., Suite 750
Washington, DC 20002
Phone: (202) 336-6700
Fax: (202) 336-6828
Email: katiec@career.org
Web: www.career.org

Carnegie Foundation for the
Advancement of Teaching
555 Middlefield Road
Menlo Park, CA 94025
Phone: (650) 566-5100
Fax: (650) 326-0278
Email: clyburn@carnegiefoundation.org
Web: www.carnegiefoundation.org

Center for Adult Learning and
Educational Credentials
American Council on Education
One Dupont Circle, N.W., Suite 250
Washington, DC 20036
Phone: (202) 939-9475
Fax: (202) 775-8578
Web: www.acenet.edu/calec/home.html

Center for the Study of Higher and
Postsecondary Education (CSHPE)
The University of Michigan - School of
Education
610 E. University
Ann Arbor, MI 48109
Phone: (313) 764-9472
Fax: (313) 764-2510
Email: cshpe.info@umich.edu
Web: www.umich.edu/~cshpe

Center on Education and Training for
Employment
Ohio State University
1900 Kenny Road
Columbus, OH 43210
Phone: (614) 292-4353
Fax: (614) 292-1260
Web: www.cete.org

College and University Personnel
Association
1233 20th St. N.W., Suite 301
Washington, DC 20036
Phone: (202) 429-0311
Fax: (202) 429-0149
Email: maitken@cupa.org
Web: www.cupa.org

Commission on Independent Colleges
and Universities
17 Elk St.
P.O. Box 7289
Albany, NY 12224
Phone: (518) 436-4781
Fax: (518) 436-0417
Email: colleges@nycolleges.org
Web: www.college-guide-nys.org

Council for Adult and Experiential
Learning
243 S. Wabash, Suite 800
Chicago, IL 60604
Phone: (312) 922-5909
Fax: (312) 922-1769
Web: www.cael.org/index2.html

Council for Advancement and Support
of Education
1307 New York Ave., N.W., Suite 1000
Washington, DC 20005
Phone: (202) 328-2273
Fax: (202) 387-4973
Email: calhoun@case.org
Web: www.case.org

Council for Christian Colleges and
Universities (CCCU)
329 Eighth St., N.E.
Washington, DC 20002
Phone: (202) 546-8713
Fax: (202) 667-8913
Web: www.gospelcom.net/cccu

Council of Graduate Schools (CGS)
One Dupont Circle, N.W., Suite 430
Washington, DC 20036
Phone: (202) 223-3791
Fax: (202) 331-7157
Web: www.cgsnet.org

Council of Independent Colleges
One Dupont Circle, N.W., Suite 320
Washington, DC 20036
Phone: (202) 466-7230
Fax: (202) 466-7238
Email: cic@cic.nche.edu
Web: www.cic.edu

Council on Foundations
1828 L. Street, N.W.
Washington, DC 20036
Phone: (202) 466-6512
Web: www.cof.org

Council on Government Relations
1200 New York Ave., N.W., Suite 320
Washington, DC 20005
Phone: (202) 289-6665
Fax: (202) 289-6698

Education Development Center
55 Chapel St.
Newton, MA 02158
Phone: (617) 969-7100
Fax: (617) 969-5979
Web: www.edc.org

Educational Resources Information
Center (ERIC)
Clearinghouse on Higher Education
One Dupont Circle, Suite 630
Washington, DC 20036
Phone: (202) 296-2597
Fax: (202) 452-1844
Email: mkozi@eric-he.edu
Web: www.eriche.org

Educational Testing Service (ETS)
Rosedale Road
Princeton, NJ 08541
Phone: (609) 921-9000
Fax: (609) 734-5410
Email: etsinfo@ets.org
Web: www.ets.org

EDUCAUSE
1112 16th Street, N.W., Suite 600
Washington, DC 20036
Phone: (202) 872-4200
Fax: (202) 872-4318
Email: info@educause.edu
Web: www.educause.edu

ERIC Clearinghouse for Community
Colleges
3051 Moore Hall, Box 951521
University of California, Los Angeles
Los Angeles, CA 90095
Phone: (800) 832-8256
Email: ericc@ucla.edu
Web: www.gseis.ucla.edu/eric/eric.html

Higher Education Processes Network
(HEPROC)
R & R Publishers, Inc.
Email: educ@heproc.org
Web: www.heproc.org

International Alliance of Teacher
Scholars
048 Pfau Library
5500 University Parkway
San Bernadino, CA 92407
Phone: (909) 880-7531
Fax: (909) 880-7532
Email: alliance@iats.com
Web: www.iats.com

International Association for
Management Education (AACSB)
600 Emerson Road, Suite 300
St. Louis, MO 63141

Phone: (314) 872-8481
Fax: (314) 872-8495
Web: www.aacsb.edu

International Council on Education for
Teaching
2009 North 14th St., Suite 609
Arlington, VA 22201
Phone: (847) 465-0191
Fax: (847) 465-5617

League for Innovation in the Community
College
26522 La Alameda, Suite 370
Mission Viejo, CA 92691
Phone: (714) 367-2884
Fax: (714) 367-2885

National Academy of Education
New York University, School of
Education
726 Broadway, 5th Floor
New York, New York 10003-9580
Phone: (212) 998-9035
Fax: (212) 995-4435
Email: nae.info@nyu.edu
Web: www.nae.nyu.edu

National Alliance of Community and
Technical Colleges
Department of Adult and Community
College Education
NC State University
300 Poe Hall, Box 7801
Raleigh, NC 27695
Web: http://admin1.athens.tec.ga.us/
nactc.html

National Association of Black
Professors
African and African-American Studies
P.O. Box 526
Christfield, MD 21827
Phone: (410) 968-2393
Email: profwood@dmv.com

National Association of College Stores
(NACS)
500 Lorain St.
Oberlin, OH 44074
Phone: (800) 622-7498
Fax: (440) 775-4769
Email: info@nacs.org
Web: www.nacs.org

National Association of Independent
Colleges and Universities (NAICU)
1025 Connecticut Ave., N.W., Suite 220
Washington, DC 20036
Phone: (202) 785-8866
Fax: (202) 835-0003
Web: www.naicu.edu

National Association of State
Universities and Land-Grant Colleges
(NASULGC)
1307 New York Ave., N.W., Suite 400
Washington, DC 20005
Phone: (202) 478-6040
Fax: (202) 478-6046
Web: www.nasulgc.org

National Association of Women in
Education
1325 18th St., N.W., Suite 210
Washington, DC 20036
Phone: (202) 659-9330
Fax: (202) 457-0946
Email: nawe@clark.net
Web: www.nawe.org

National Center for Education Statistics
555 New Jersey Ave., N.W.
Washington, DC 20208
Phone: (202) 219-1828
Web: www.nces.ed.gov

National Center for Research in
Vocational Education (NCRVE)
University of California, Berkeley
2030 Addison St., Suite 500
Berkeley, CA 94720
Phone: (800) 762-4093
Email: Askncrve@ncrve.berkeley.edu
Web: http://vocserve.berkeley.edu/
brochure.html

National Collegiate Athletic Association
6201 College Blvd.
Overland Parkf, KS 66211
Phone: (913) 339-1906
Fax: (913) 339-0038
Web: www.ncaa.org

National Association for Women in
Education (NAWE)
1325 18th St., N.W., Suite 210
Washington, DC 20036
Phone: (202) 659-9330
Fax: (202) 457-0946
Web: www.nawe.org

National Education Association
1201 16th St., N.W.
Washington, DC 20036
Phone: (202) 833-4000
Fax: (202) 822-7642
Web: www.nea.org/he

National Education Knowledge Industry
Association (NEKIA)
1200 19th St., N.W., Suite 300
Washington, DC 20036
Phone: (202) 429-5101
Fax: (202) 785-3894
Web: www.cedar.org

National Institute on Postsecondary
Education, Libraries, and Lifelong
Learning (PLLI)
U.S. Department of Education
555 New Jersey Ave., N.W.
Washington, DC 20208
Phone: (202) 219-2207
Fax: (202) 501-3005
Web: www.ed.gov/offices/OERI/PLLI/
phpsee.html

National Library of Education
U.S. Department of Education (DOE)
400 Maryland Ave. S.W.
Washington, DC 20202
Phone: (800) 424-1616
Fax: (202) 401-0552
Email: library@ed.gov
Web: www.ed.gov/nle

Office of Postsecondary Education
Department of Education
1990 K Street, N.W.
Washington, DC 20006
Web: www.ed.gov/offices/ope

Office of Vocational & Adult Education
Department of Education
4090 MES
400 Maryland Ave., S.W.
Washington, DC 20202
Phone: (202) 205-5451
Fax: (202) 205-8748
Email: ovae@inet.ed.gov
Web: www.ed.gov/offices/ovae

U.S. Department of Education
400 Maryland Avenue, S.W.
Washington, DC 20202
Phone: (800) 872-5327
Web: www.ed.gov

University Continuing Education
Association
One Dupont Circle, N.W., Suite 615
Washington, DC 20036
Phone: (202) 659-3130
Fax: (202) 785-0374
Web: www.nucea.edu

Washington Higher Education
  Secretariat (WHES)
One Dupont Circle, N.W., Suite 800
Washington, DC 20036
Phone: (202) 939-9345
Fax: (202) 833-4723
Web: www.whes.org

Reference Books and Bibliography

*Adjunct Professor's Guide to Success,
Surviving and Thriving in the College
Classroom,* 1999, Lyons, R., Kysilka, M,
Pawlas, G., Allyn & Bacon, Needham
Heights, MA

*American Freshman: National Norms for
Fall 1998,* 1998, Sax, L.J., Astin, A.W.,
Korn, W.S. & Mahoney, K.M., Higher
Education Research Institute, UCLA
Graduate School of Education and
Information Studies, Los Angeles, CA

*Extending the Classroom Walls
Electronically,* 1996, Creed, T.,
Interaction Book Company, Edina, MN

*Fall Staff in Postsecondary Institutions,
1995,* 1998, Roey, S., Rak, R.,
Fernandez, R., Barbett, S., National
Center for Education Statistics - U.S.
Department of Education, Washington,
DC

*Handbook for Adjunct and Part-time
Faculty (A),* 1984, 6th edition, Grieve, D.,
INFO-TEC, Inc., Cleveland

*Handbook for New College Teachers
and Teaching Assistants,* 1992, Davis,
C., Davis & Associates

*Handbook of College Teaching, Theory
and Applications,* 1994, Editors:
Prichard, K., Sawyer, M., Greenwood
Press, Westport, CT

*Handbook of Procedures for the Design
of Instruction,* 1981, 2nd Edition, Briggs,
L., Wager, W., Educational Technology
Publications, Inc.

*Handbook for Teachers in Universities &
Colleges (A), A Guide to Improving
Teaching Methods,* 1989, 1st edition,
Newble, D., Cannon, R., St. Martin's
Press, New York

*How To Turn Learners on Without
Turning Them Off, Ways To Ignite
Interest in Learning,* 1997, 3rd edition,
Mager, R., Center for Effective
Performance, Inc.

*Making Instruction Work, A Step-by-
Step Guide to Designing & Developing
Instruction That Works,* 1997, Mager,
R., Center for Effective Performance,
Inc.

Principles of Instructional Design, 1992,
4th edition, Gagne, R., Holt, Rheinhart &
Winston School Division

*(The) Professor Business, A Teaching
Primer for Faculty,* 1990, Flood, B.,
Moll, J., Learned Information, Inc.,
Medford, NJ

*Quick Hits, Successful Strategies by
Award Winning Teachers,* 1994, editors:
Bender, E., Dunn, M., Kendall, B.,
Larson, C., Wilkes, P., Indiana
University Press, Bloomington

Systematic Design of Instruction, 1996,
4th edition, Dick, W., Carey, L., Addison-
Wesley Educational Publishers, Inc.

*Teaching at Its Best, A Research-Based
Resource for College Instructors,* 1998,
Nilson, L., Anker Publishing Company,
Inc., Bolton, MA

*Teaching Strategies & Techniques for
Adjunct Faculty,* 1991, 2nd Edition,
Greive, D., INFO-TEC Inc., Cleveland

Teaching With Style, A Practical Guide to Enhancing Learning by UnderstandingTeaching and Learning Styles, 1996, Grasha, A., Alliance Publishers, Pittsburg

Teaching Within the Rhythms of the Semester, 1995, Duffy, D., Jones, J., Jossey-Bass Publishers, San Francisco

Magazines, Newsletters and Journals

American Journal of Education
The University of Chicago Press
The University of Chicago
Judd Hall #305
5835 S. Kimbark Ave.
Chicago, IL 60637
Phone: (773) 753-3347
Fax: (773) 753-0811
Web: www.journals.uchicago.edu/
  aje/home.html

The Chronicle of Higher Education
1255 23rd. St. N.W.
Washington, DC 20037
Phone: (800) 728-2803
Fax: (202) 223-6292
Web: www.chronicle.com

Journal of College Science Teaching
National Science Teachers Association
1840 Wilson Blvd.
Arlington, VA 22201
Phone: (703) 243-7100
Fax: (703) 243 7177
Email: Michael.Byrnes@nsta.org
Web: www.nsta.org

Journal of Teaching in International
  Business
The Haworth Press
10 Alice St.
Binghamton, NY 13904
Phone: (800) 429-6784
Fax: (800) 895-0582
Web: www.haworth.com

On the Horizon (on-line)
Jossey-Bass Publishers
350 Sansome St.
San Francisco, CA 94104
Web: http://horizon.unc.edu/horizon

Presentations Magazine
Lakewood Publications
50 S. Ninth St.
Minneapolis, MN 55402
Phone: (612) 333-0471
Fax: (612) 333-6562
Email: rganzel@presentations.com
Web: www.presentations.com

Project MUSE (on-line)
Scholarly Journals On-line
http://muse.jhu.edu/

Stanford University's Newsletter on
  Teaching
Center for Teaching and Learning -
Stanford University
Phone: (650) 723-1326
Web: www-ctl.stanford.edu

Syllabus Magazine
345 Northlake Drive
San Jose, CA 95117
Phone: (408) 261-7200
Fax: (408) 261-7280
Email: info@syllabus.com
Web: www.syllabus.com

Tech Directions
3970 Varsity Drive
Ann Arbor, MI 48108
Phone: (734) 975-2800
Fax (734) 975-2787
Web: www.techdirections.com

TECHniques Magazine
Association for Career and Technical
Education (ACTE)
1410 King St.
Alexandria, VA 22314
Phone: (800) 826-9972
Fax: (703) 683-7424
Email: acte@acteonline.org
Web: www.avaonline.org

T.H.E. Journal (Technological Horizons
  in Education) & T.H.E. Journal On-line
17501 E. 17th St., Suite 230
Tustin, CA 92780
Phone: (714) 730-4011
Web: www.thejournal.com

The Review of Higher Education
Johns Hopkins University Press
P.O. Box 19966
Baltimore, MD 21211
Phone: (800) 548-1784
Fax: (410) 516-6908
Web: www.press.jhu.edu

International Resources

Association of International Educators
  (NAFSA)
1875 Connecticut Ave. N.W., Suite 1000
Washington, DC 200009
USA
Phone: (202) 426-4811
Fax: (202) 667-3419
Web: www.nafsa.org

Association of University Teachers
Egmont House
25-31 Tavistock Place
London, WC1H 9UT
ENGLAND
Phone: +44 1 71 670 9700
Fax: +44 1 71 670 9799
Email: hq@aut.org.uk
Web: www.aut.org.uk

Boston College Center for International
  Higher Education
207 Campion Hall
School of Education, Boston College
Chestnut Hill, MA 0216
USA
Phone: (617) 552-4236
Fax: (617) 552-8422
Web: www.bc.edu/bc_org/avp/soe/
    cihe/Center1.html

Council for International Exchange of
  Scholars (CIES)
3007 Tilden St., N.W., Suite 5L
Washington, DC 20008
USA
Phone: (202) 686-4000
Fax: (202) 362-3442
Email: info@ciesnet.cies.org
Web: www.iie.org/cies/

Central Intelligence Agency
Country Data (On-line)
Washington, DC
USA
Web: www.odci.gov/cia/publications/
    factbook/index.html

European Association for International
  Education
P.O. Box 11189
GD Amsterdam, 1001
NETHERLANDS
Phone: +31-20-525 4999
Fax: +31-20-525 4998
Email: eaie@eaie.nl
Web: www.eaie.nl

Distance Learning Association
European Association of Distance
  Learning Universities (EADTU)
Valkenburgerweg 177
AT Heerlen, 6419
NETHERLANDS
Phone: +31 45 5762214
Fax: +31 45 5741473
Email: niek.pronk@eadtu.nl
Web: www.eadtu.nl

First Year on Campus
Center for the Study of Higher
  Education
University of Melbourne
Melbourne
AUSTRALIA
Web: www.cshe.unimelb.edu.au

Institute of International Education (IIE)
809 United Nations Plaza
New York, NY 10017
Phone: (212) 984-5400
Fax: (212) 984-5452
Web: www.iie.org

Instructional Technology
Human Resources Development
Office of Learning Technologies
CANADA
Web: http://olt-bta.hrdc-drhc.gc.ca

International Associations of
  Universities
Unesco House
1, rue Miollis
Paris - Cedex 15, 75732
FRANCE
Phone: +33 (1) 45 68 25 45
Fax: +33 (1) 47 34 76 05
Email: iau@unesco.org
Web: www.unesco.org/iau

International Forum of Educational
Technology & Society
c/o Dr. Kinshuk
GMD-FIT Schloss Birlinghoven
Sankt Augustin, 53754
GERMANY
Phone: +49 2241 14 2144
Fax: +49 2241 14 2065
Web: http://ifets.gmd.de

Corporate Support
Microsoft (International)
USA
Web: www.microsoft.com/education/
world.asp

Teaching Support Organization
Society for Teaching and Learning in
Higher Education (STLHE)
c/o Centre for the Support of Teaching,
York University
4700 Keele St.
North York, Ontario M3J 1P3
CANADA
Phone: (416) 736-5009
Fax: (416) 736-5913
Email: rzeszute@cc.umanitoba.ca
Web: www.umanitoba.ca/academic_
support/uts/stlhe/general.html

Organization for Educational
Development
The International Consortium of
Educational Development
The Oxford Centre for Staff
Development
Oxford Brooks University
Headington, Oxford OX3 0BP
ENGLAND
Phone: +44 1 865 750918.
Fax: +44 1 865 744437
Email: f.lam@brookes.ac.uk
Web:www.abo.fi/instut/hied/iced.
htm#details

Newspaper Support
The Times Higher Education
Supplement
Admiral House
66-68 E. Smithfield
London, E1 8XY
ENGLAND
Phone: +44 171 782 3000
Fax: +44 171 782 3300
Email: theschat@thes.co.uk
Web: www.thesis.co.uk

Educational Magazine
University Affairs
Association of Universities and Colleges
of Canada
600-350 Albert St.
Ottawa, Ontario K1R 1B1
CANADA
Phone: (613) 563-1236
Fax: (613) 563-9745
Email: pberkowi@aacc.ca
Web: www.aucc.ca

Textbook Publishers (selected list)

Addison-Wesley Longman (Higher
Education)
One Jacob Way
Reading, MA 01867
Phone: (781) 944-3700
Fax: (781) 944-9338
Web: www.awl.com

Bedford/St.Martin's Publishing
345 Park Ave. S., 6th floor
New York, NY 10010
Phone: (800) 470-4767
Fax: (212) 686-9492
Email: facultyservices@sasmp.com
Web: www.bedfordstmartins.com

Benjamin/Cummings Science
Addison Wesley Longman, Inc.
One Jacob Way
Reading, MA 01867
Phone: (781) 944-3700
Fax: (781) 944-9338
Web: www.awl.com

Blackwell Publishers, Inc.
350 Malden St.
Malden, MA 02148
Phone: (781) 388-8200
Fax: (781) 388-8210
Email: ranni@blackwellpub.com
Web: www.blackwellpublishers.co.uk

Dryden Press
301 Commerce St., Suite 3700
Fort Worth, TX 76102
Phone: (817) 334-7500
Web: www.dryden.com

Holt, Rinehart & Winston
1120 S. Capital St.
Austin, TX 78746
Phone: (800) 479-9799
Web: www.harcourt.com

Houghton Mifflin
College Division
222 Berkeley St.
Boston, MA 02116
Phone: (617) 351-5000
Web: www.hmco.com

International Thompson Press (ITP)
The Metro Center
One Station Place, 6th Floor
Stamford, CT 06902
Phone: (203) 328-9400
Fax: (203) 328-9408
Web: www.itp.thomson.com

Jossey-Bass Publishing
350 Sansome St.
San Franscisco, CA 94101
Phone: (415) 433-1740
Fax: (415) 433-0499
Email: webperson@jbp.com
Web: www.josseybass.com

McGraw-Hill (Higher Education)
1333 Burr Ridge Parkway
Burr Ridge, IL 60521
Phone: (800) 262-4729
Fax: (614) 759-3644
Email: customer.service@mcgraw-hill.com
Web: www.mhhe.com

Oxford University Press
198 Madison Avenue
New York, NY 10016
Phone: (212) 726-6000
Fax: (212) 726-6440
Web: www.oup-usa.org

Prentice Hall - Faculty Services
One Lake St.
Upper Saddle River, NJ 07458
Phone: (800) 526-0485
Web: www.phdirect.com

Saunders College Publishing
The Public Ledger Building, Suite 1250
150 S. Independence Mall W.
Philadelphia, PA 19106

Phone: (215) 238-5500
Web: www.harcourt.com

W. H. Freeman and Company
c/o Von Holtzbrinck Publishing Services
16365 James Madison Highway
Gordonsville, VA 22942
Phone: (888) 330-8477
Fax: (800) 672-2054
Web: www.whfreeman.com

Worth Publishers Inc.
Faculty Services
33 Irving Place
New York, NY 10003
Phone: (800) 446-8923
Fax: (212) 995-8923
Email: facultyservices@bfwpub.com
Web: www.worthpublishers.com

Teaching Centers (selected list)

Center for Academic Excellence
Portland State University
Web: www.oaa.pdx.edu/cae

Center for Excellence in Learning and Teaching
Penn State University
Web: www.psu.edu/celt

Center for Teaching and Learning
Stanford University
Web: www-ctl.stanford.edu/

Center for Teaching Excellence
University of Kansas
Web: http://eagle.cc.ukans.edu/~cte/index.html

Center for Teaching Excellence
University of North Carolina - Wilmington
Web: http://cte.uncwil.edu

Eberly Center for Teaching Excellence
Carnegie Mellon University
Web: www.cmu.edu/provost/teaching

Maricopa Center for Learning and Instruction (MCLI)
Maricopa Community College
Web: www.mcli.dist.maricopa.edu/cc/info.html

Office of Instructional Development and
  Technology
Dalhousie University
Web: http://is.dal.ca/~oidt

Office of Teaching Effectiveness
University of Colorado at Denver
Web: www.cudenver.edu/public/ote

Program for Excellence in Teaching
University of Missouri
Columbia, MO 65211
Phone: (573) 882-6260
Fax: (573) 884-4690
Email: pet@missouri.edu
Web: http://web.missouri.edu/
  ~petwww/

University Center for Teaching and
  Learning
Cleveland State University
Web: www.csuohio.edu:80/uctl/
  links.html

University Teaching & Learning Center
University of North Carolina,
  Greensboro
Web: www.uncg.edu/tlc

Internet Links in Higher Education

Canadian Association for University
  Continuing Education
Web: http://cauce-aepuc.ca/English/
  links/

Charles Stewart University Education
  Virtual Library
Web: http://lorenz.mur.csu.edu.au/
  education/tertiary.html

Distance Learning Sites
Web: www-net.com/univ/list/
  distance.html

Ed Links - Marshall
Web: www.webpages.marshall.edu
  ~jmullens/edlinks.html

Educational Associations on the Internet
Horizon
Web: http://horizon.unc.edu/onramp/
  associations.asp

Effective Teaching Cybrary
University of North Carolina, Wilmington
Web: http://cte.uncwil.edu/et/
  cybrary.htm

Article: Getting Started (Felder & Brent)
Web: www2.ncsu.edu/unity/lockers/
  users/f/felder/public/Columns/
  Getstart.html

Jossey-Bass Links
Web: www.JosseyBass.com/links.shtml

Article: Learning Styles (R.M. Felder)
Web:www2.ncsu.edu/unity/lockers/
  users/f/felder/public/
  Learning_Styles.html

Library of Congress (U.S.)
Web: www.loc.gov

National Association for Diversity
  Management (NADM)
Web: www.nadm.org

National Association of State
  Universities and Land-Grant Colleges
Web: www.nasulgc.nche.edu/useful.htm

New York City Literacy Assistance
  Center
Web: www.lacnyc.org/links/index.html

Online University Teaching Centers
  (US)
Center for Teaching Excellence
University of Kansas
Web: http://eagle.cc.ukans.edu/~cte/
  educationalsites.html

OSCN Education and Training
  (Employment Center)
Web: http://bcn.boulder.co.us/oscn/
  educ-train/edtrain.html

Scholarly Societies Project
Univerity of Waterloo (Canada)
Web: www.lib.uwaterloo.ca/society/
  education_soc.html

Teaching and Learning Center
University of North Carolina –
Greensboro
Website: www.uncg.edu/tlc/

Teaching and Learning Sites in Higher
Education
Dalhousie University
Web: http://is.dal.ca/~oidt/other.html

(Dr.) Tom Creed's Web Site
St. John's University
Collegeville, MN 56321
Web: www.users.csbsju.edu\~tcreed

University Center for Teaching and
Learning
Cleveland State University
Web: www.csuohio.edu:80/
    uctl/links.html

Washington Higher Education
    Secretariat (WHES)
Web: www.whes.org/members.
    index.html

Other Resources

Association of Educational Publishers
Rowan University
201 Mullica Hill Road
Glassboro, NJ 08028
Phone: (609) 256-4610
Fax: (609) 256-4926
Email: edpress@aol.com
Web: www.edpress.org

Peterson's Publishing
Reference Books
202 Carnegie Center
Princeton, NJ 08540
Phone: (800) 338-3282
Fax: (609) 243-9111
Email: custsvc@petersons.com
Web: www.petersons.com

University of California - Instructional
    Consultation
Information on Legal Considerations in
    Higher Education
Web: www.id.ucsb.edu/ic/resources/
    teaching/legal/intro.html

The Lilly Conference on College and
    University Teaching (regional teaching
    enhancement conferences held
    throughout the year)
Web: www.iats.com

Syllabus Conferences (regional and
    national conferences focussing on
    instructional technology in higher ed)
Web: www.syllabus.com

INDEX

ORDER & CONTACT FORM

To order a copy of *The Teaching Bridge, a Resource Manual for Part-Time Teachers in Today's Colleges and Universities,* photocopy the order form below and mail it with <u>check</u> or <u>money order</u> to:

**Arizona Mission Press
P.O. Box 28
Davidson, NC 28036-0028**

I would like:

❑ To order the manual:

_____ x $29.95 each (1 – 5 copies)

_____ x $24.95 each (6 copies or more)

Total amount enclosed: $ _____

Delivery: Please allow two to three weeks for delivery.

❑ To suggest updates/additions for future manuals (please attach).

❑ Other: _____

Name: _____

School: _____

Address: _____

_____

Phone: (   ) _____ Email: _____

ADDITIONAL NOTES